How to Be the Girl Who

Gets the Guy

How Irresistible, Confident and Self-Assured Women

Handle Dating with Class and Sass

Written by Leslie Braswell

Printed by Kindle Direct Publishing,
An Amazon.com Company

Available from Amazon.com and other bookstores

Also available on Audible, Kindle and other devices

DISCLAIMER AND LEGAL NOTICES

The information presented and contained herein represents the view of the author as of the date of this publication. The Author reserves the right to change her opinions based on new information at any time.

The material is general dating advice only and is not intended to be a substitute for professional, medical or psychological advice and counseling.

Dedicated to my family. You're my favorite people.

Table of Contents

Introduction

My hope is as you read this book, you experience a significant increase in your confidence and raise your standards in the process. Throughout this book, I refer to confident women, self-assured women, and self-made women. I'm not referring to confident women who are arrogant, proud, or selfish. But instead, women who are self-reliant, unpretentious, classy, and kind. These are the women who have acquired a quiet inner strength we all strive to possess. Real confidence evolves over a period of time. It comes from a growing belief you can rely on, provide for, and love yourself under any given set of circumstances. Everyone has the potential to raise their confidence level and increase their sense of self-worth.

Many women are born with confidence, while so many others simply are not. If you are *not* blessed with confidence, it is time to learn what some of the most beautiful starlets who ever graced the silver screen did. *Fake it.* Yes, yes, that's right - fake it till you make it. I am not asking you to steer away from being your genuine, authentic self. I am asking you to train yourself to *be* confident. Fine-tune a few behaviors we are all guilty of committing. And learn to love yourself more than ever.

We've all made mistakes when it comes to matters of the heart. We must chalk our past dating mistakes up to a learning experience and use them to our advantage for future relationships… We must use them to help other women. Because that's what classy women do, we help our sisters. Mistakes you make in the dating arena are just a natural part of life. We can't dwell on the blunders of boyfriends' past. We can't be afraid to fail. We can't be scared to try. Some women make the same mistakes over and over and over. Great women learn from their mistakes and move on. We must adopt the mindset when one door closes another bigger, better door opens to a brighter dating future with a bigger, better love.

Jim Rohn once said, "Happiness is not something you postpone for the future; it is something you design for the present." Only you can create and make new things happen in your life for the better. While others wait for fate or serendipity to step in to provide a beautiful life, you will be one step ahead of the game by creating one. The confident woman knows the path to happiness is her responsibility to find. She isn't postponing her joy, waiting for Mr. Right to provide it to her. Instead, she is taking hold of the reins and going with her instincts.

Rest assured, no one is entirely confident in all areas of their life. Every woman has insecurities which plague her mind and continually creep up at the most inopportune time. However, if little by little you convey confidence each day, if you tweak a few of your behavior patterns to lean toward confidence, you eventually become the amazing, confident woman God created you to be. By envisioning and planning for the life you want for yourself. By knowing who you are, regardless if a man is in your life on a temporary basis, a permanent one, or, not at all.

It is perfectly normal to *want* to put your best face on in the early phases of a relationship. But hiding behind a veil will only get you so far. And for a relationship to last for the long haul, you must be the real you – an original, authentic, one of a kind masterpiece. It's all about the way you present yourself to the world. If you have confidence, you can have just about any man you choose. You can be *The Girl Who Gets the Guy.*

Chapter 1

Sexier Than a Great Pair of Legs

"A dame that knows the ropes isn't likely to get tied up."

-- Mae West

Silver screen goddesses struggle with it, Super Models crave it, and Marilyn Monroe, arguably the sexiest woman of all time, could not obtain it. If only we were born with it. If I could manufacture and sell it in a 1.5 fluid ounce bottle, Oprah would indeed deem it to be one of her favorite things. No one can be *it* twenty-four hours a day, seven days a week. The best-selling self-help books on Amazon cannot instantly make you possess it. (Although it is an excellent place to start.)

I'm talking about the thing men call sexier than a great pair of legs. *Confidence.* You can't touch it, but you can certainly feel it. You don't have to be a size two to project it. Beauty comes in any size if you're confident. What I want you to go away with after reading this book is how to escalate your worth in the eyes of any man. It all starts with one simple thing. *You.* Whether you are single, divorced, widowed, married, in a complicated relationship or no relationship at all, depicting yourself as a high-value woman of worth who has the three C's... Character, confidence, and charm. Add a touch of dignity, and a man will be wrapped around your pedicured pinky finger. Because when you believe in yourself, others believe in you as well. A man simply can't fall in love with a woman who does not love or respect herself.

It's no wonder why we all struggle with confidence throughout our lives. We tend to overlook the best of ourselves and focus on our most critical inadequacies. We fret over our abilities regardless of how accomplished or successful we are. We believe the never silent, inner voice whispering in our ears, telling us we are not good enough. We must learn to tell that voice to *shut the hell up.* We must find a way to mute the negative inner voice that tells us we're not good enough.

Too many women believe they will only be perceived as beautiful, based on their outer beauty or sex appeal. *Nonsense!* Men are not on the lookout for a supermodel. -- Except Leonardo DiCaprio, but I'm not talking about him. *Instead,* I'm referring to the rest of the male population. Looks play a major factor for men, but it's not the *deciding* factor. Plenty of wedding venues are booked every year well in advance for plain, ordinary, below-average women.

Through media, we are inundated with airbrushed images of women with flawless skin and voluminous hair. Even though we are equally aware, an expert photoshopper has shaved inches off their thighs and waists, and hair extensions have been strategically placed by a team of guys and gals who earn their living making women look fabulous. The media puts too much pressure on women as to what it takes to become what the ideal woman should be. The fact is, it is out of our reach. It's unobtainable. The average woman could never become what the ad executives have projected the "perfect woman" to look like because it is their edited, airbrushed version of perfection. In an interview with Refinery29, Blake Lively said something that I hope every woman recognizes. She said, "We have really unrealistic beauty standards and beauty norms. What you're seeing on red carpets and in magazines takes a lot of effort and a lot of people. People don't understand that it's all very constructed. What little girls are seeing ISN'T what [these celebrities] look like when they wake up in the morning — even though it's no less beautiful." My version of beautiful is doing the best you can for yourself, your family, and friends every single day. If you do that, what more could you ask of yourself?

Often, the beliefs that occupy space in our brains focus on imperfections in our appearance, which only exist in our minds. The fact is, beauty is far beyond skin deep. As one man said, "The larger woman who walks into a room with confidence and communicates with humor *and* who is self-assured, I love that woman." His message: Stop focusing on your imperfections and start focusing on what makes you uniquely you. Personality is sexy as hell.

Confidence Is Like a Muscle:
The More You Use It, The Stronger And Sexier It Gets

There are ways in which you can reprogram your brain over time to retrain the way you think about yourself. For every negative thought which enters your mind, have positive thoughts on standby to rebuff them. *"I'm amazing, I'm caring, I'm thoughtful, and I'm kind."* Just as you exercise to shape your body, you can change the way you view yourself. Your brain changes based on what you do and how you think. Every day add a new positive thought to your collection. Make a list either mentally or on paper of all your qualities, things you're good at, and personal achievements. Read and reread until they are ingrained in your mind. As you walk down the street or into an office, silently repeat over and over to yourself and walk with a smile on your face.

Time and time again, you will hear men describe confidence as the sexiest characteristic a woman can possess. Confidence is the core of so many attractive qualities. A sense of humor, kindness, compassion, and a woman who has her life together. Think of the way women in a James Bond movie portray themselves on the silver screen to play the part of a Bond girl. Pilant and undemanding, beautiful but innocent, outdoorsy, physically tough, covertly vulnerable, and uncomplaining.

A top-notch man wants a top-notch woman. Good looks may get you in the door, but they won't keep you there. A woman doesn't have to have Jennifer Lopez's good looks or hair down to her waist. After he likes what he sees, the next thing on his list is to find out if you are fun, sweet, trustworthy, responsible, honest, and finally, *kind*. She is the girl who meets dear sweet mom. Notice what was not on the list: Clingy, needy, desperate, and a total demanding bitch.

For every man, there is at least one woman who possesses all the qualities that make up the "it" factor that appeals to him. There is no rhyme or reason as to why one man may be attracted to one woman over another... other than one is more interesting and put together. The "it girl" must be beautiful in his eyes; she possesses sex appeal without being pompous. "It" is indescribable.

If You Look Pretty, You'll Feel Pretty

French Fashion Designer, Coco Chanel once said, "Dress shabbily, they notice the dress. Dress impeccably, and they remember the woman." The same should be true for the way you present yourself to the world each day. It is a fact woman who work in professional office settings, who wear makeup and dress professionally, make more money than those who do not. If this holds true in the world of business, it only makes sense the same is true in the love department. Dress each day as if you are going to meet Mr. Right. I believe this to be true for one simple reason: While sitting at my desk one morning many years ago, the door opened and in walked a handsome, well-dressed man. I didn't know it then, but years later, I call that man my husband. Had you told me I would one day be married to him; I would have had a good laugh. We were friends for the longest time, and eventually, he asked me out for lunch. And on the lunch list is where he stayed for at least a year or more before our first date. The point is: You never know where cupid's arrow is pointing and on whom it will land. So, each day dress to impress but dress true to yourself. Wear what makes you feel beautiful, confident, and self-assured.

Being visual creatures, they notice if you are doing the best you can with what you have to work with. Each morning, before you leave your home, get dressed for the rest of the day. Be done with it. You'll feel good about yourself for the remainder of the day.

Do you think you have to spend a fortune on makeup? If so, think again. There is not a drugstore in America that won't enhance a woman's appearance even on a shoestring budget. Your local drugstore is the home to CoverGirl makeup, which has been perfectly good enough to be applied to the beautiful faces of Pink, Rihanna, Drew Barrymore, Cybill Shepherd, Ellen DeGeneres, Queen Latifah, Taylor Swift, and let's not forget Christie Brinkley. She has been the CoverGirl model/spokeswoman for at least half of your life, or since you were born. Here is my point: For forty bucks or less, you can have a whole new fabulous look.

The reality is we are judged based on looks. Men place significant importance on physical beauty. So, before you walk out of your home each morning, put forth the effort to look your best. Which, in turn, will boost your confidence level. Which will make a man's head spin in your direction. While passing him on the street, what will his first thought be? "WOW, look at that beautiful lady," or "poor thing, she's probably homeless." Men can tell within the first ninety seconds of meeting a woman if he is interested in her or not. Within 30 minutes, they've made long-term conclusions about your character. First impressions count!

Chances are a man would not ask you out, or date you at all if he did not believe you were easy on the eyes. To a man, looks are a major factor, but they're not the only factor. Men aren't entirely shallow. A friend of mine ran out of gas while mowing her yard. She pulled up to the gas station with no makeup, her hair in a ball cap, sweaty with grass shavings on her legs. When a guy who was filling up his truck next to her appeared and asked if he could help, she happily accepted. Before she left, he had asked her out on a date. She couldn't say no to a man who asked her out while she looked her worst. The point is each man has their version of what beauty is.

Some are into super skinny like Taylor Swift, while others love a full figure, like Mellissa McCarthy. Some men are into women who have a muscular build, while others prefer women with more cushion. If a man were to give you a hard time about your appearance, I hope you use your lady's brain and have enough common sense to put him in his place or remove him from your life at once.

Body issues can be brutal for women who have had children and are insecure about their bodies. You've probably disclosed you have kids to anyone you are dating. Simply because bragging about their kiddos is what good mamas do. If you've had one or even four children, a man has no expectation for your breasts to be perfect and perky or your abs to be rock hard. So, own your body and love it.

If you feel the need to work out more, to feel empowered and sexy, then work out. But at the end of the day, you must accept and believe your body is a temple and stop giving a shit about what anyone may think. When a confident woman decides to change something about her body or her appearance, she does so for herself. She does not conform to what another's version of beauty is.

Confidence is derived from many sources. However, women should always feel confident in their intelligence. It's not necessarily about being book smart or having a Master's Degree. Confidence comes from instincts, intuition, insight, common sense, street smarts, and emotional intelligence. Even the most confident women have weaknesses, but they don't dwell on them. Instead, they find ways to accentuate their strengths. Train yourself to put your efforts into focusing on the good attributes you have and work them all to your advantage. Be confident in yourself and the decisions you make. I am not suggesting putting forth the effort to enhance your appearance is not important. I would rather you show up late *than ugly*. However, it is just as important to work on your inner beauty because what is on the inside is what will ultimately win a man's heart. The beautiful qualities you possess within are what sets you apart and makes you one of a kind.

A Confident Woman Can Fly Solo

Do you mind buying lunch for one or catching a movie on your own? Do you worry about what others will think if they see you alone? If so, you're overthinking.

Whether walking into a room or out on a date, do so with your chin up *(your nose shouldn't be too high in the air)*, head upward, shoulders back, and make eye contact with every person you encounter, and always have a smile on your face. Walk as if three men are walking behind you.

Never Be a Snob to New Endeavors or New Men

Consider life as one big experiment. Never turn your nose up at experimenting with the unknown. *(Except for hotels, then be a snob.)* Men want to date women who have life experiences, and the only way you will gain experience is if, at every opportunity available, you try something new. Start small if you must but do something. Is there a new restaurant you want to try? Treat yourself to dinner for one. Is there something you have always been interested in, but too afraid to try? Take a class to learn about it. Don't be scared to go out by yourself. You might be surprised by the new friends you may meet.

A woman I know loved to create women's scarfs, socks, hand warmers, and hair accessories with knits. She combined her love of lace and knits and turned it into a line of knitwear accessories. What started out as a hobby, working at her kitchen table, is now one of the most prosperous shops on Etsy. She sells over three thousand items every day. Her then-boyfriend, now-husband, didn't blink an eye before rolling up his sleeves to help her grow her business.

Relationships Start with Good Conversation

The art of conversation is knowing how to start one. Something as simple as "hello" is a terrific place to start. I'm not promising it will get you a date, but it could. Make eye contact with at least ten men a day and say "hi" every chance you can. Some may look at you like you're from another planet, but one may take notice. You may meet a man who is impolite and unfriendly. He may already be in a committed relationship, or he's just not interested in you. *No harm, no foul.* You only need to turn one head.

I'm not trying to convince you that you can have *any* man you want. You simply can't. There is no magic love spell or love fragrance that will lure any man you want into your arms. Rejection is a part of life. There is simply no way to sugar coat it. It still doesn't matter because, at the end of the day, we all want to try for love. The mission for love is what keeps people going.

No need to start conversations with flirty lines, your past wretched love history, the horrible divorce you're going through, or demean yourself by using calculating emotional schemes. Just try and have a conversation, get to know him. There is also no need to lead with romance, love, or sex. He'll think you are too "eager" and show you what a great athlete he can be by showing you how fast he can run.

Attract them with shared interests and engaging, pleasant conversation. Men tend to fall for women who share common interests. Someone they can relate to on a personal level. Those are the women they seek a relationship with. Until then, you are placed in one of two categories:

Category One: I would sleep with her.

Category Two: I would *not* sleep with her.

Based on which category you have been placed, a man will nicely brush you off, or he will start planning ways to lure you to his lair. If you keep the topic of sex or the act of sex out of the equation, the more time and energy he'll dedicate to persuading you, he's a great guy.

There are two other categories a man will place you in. The first is his "Reserve List," and the second is his "Marriage Material List."

The Reserve List is made up of women who he will make the least effort to sleep with and place on a rotation. His goal is to see if you are a cheap date, meaning he wants to know if he can get you drunk quickly. If all you are interested in is "just sex," you're good to go. This man may be just what the doctor ordered. Maybe you're so busy with work you don't have time for relationships or men who want *more*. Perhaps you are at a place in life where you don't want a man. (Been there, done that.) Maybe "just sex" suits your lifestyle just fine. No judgment passed.

However, if you would like to be placed in the second category, "Marriage Material," don't give him everything he wants, *too soon*. You'll know soon enough if you are on this list because of his actions. He'll introduce you to his friends, take you out on real dates, he'll let you know throughout the day you're on his mind. This man will never put doubt in your mind. You'll never wonder when your next date will be because he's two steps ahead of the game. He views his "job" is to make you happy.

Date Night Tips

➜ *Pretty is as pretty does.* Your looks may get you the first date, but they won't guarantee you a second or third. So, remember the "It girl" is the complete package. She possesses inner beauty, which enhances her outer beauty.

➜ *Gracefully Accept Compliments.* When a man tells you how beautiful you are, a simple "thank you" works nicely. Don't talk him out of the compliment by disagreeing. Each day, remind yourself -

- You are remarkable.
- You are lovely.
- You are valued.
- You are important.
- You are special.
- You are unique.
- You are compassionate; and
- You are loved.

It's also a good idea *not* to fish for compliments. For example, don't ask, "Do I look okay?" "Do you like my outfit?" or, "Do you think I am pretty?" Self-assured women do not seek or require validation about their appearance.

→ ***Don't Reveal Too Much, Too Soon.*** Leave your childhood problems, daddy issues, and dating drama buried in the past. What matters, in the beginning, is that you present yourself in the most flattering light. There is no need to share every single detail of your life, no matter how routine or private in the early stages. *Remember,* some things should only be divulged to your best friend, therapist, or lawyer.

Revealing too much, too soon, takes away from a woman's mystery. I'm not asking you to lie; I'm asking you to take things slowly and let him fall in love with the beautiful woman you are *without* issues. You can gently disclose difficulties later and in small increments, over time.

There is a difference between insecurity and vulnerability. Being vulnerable allows you to reveal yourself without holding back for fear of rejection. Instead of telling every single one of your weaknesses on the first date, do so over a period. If you reveal you've lived through the curveball's life has thrown at you, it reveals you have an, "I'm still standing" mindset.

On the first few dates, a man is trying to figure out your hidden agenda. He wants to know if you're trying to snag a man. Sidestep topics that center around your future family plans for marriage, babies, or your list of requirements.

→ *Never discuss Ghosts of Boyfriends Past.* Discussing former flames serves no real purpose and can do more harm than good. Leave your dating past, in the past. If you continually speak about Mr. Ex, it reveals you are still thinking of him. It's not informative or fun for the other person, and it doesn't make you more appealing. And he will wonder if you are genuinely over Mr. Ex. Before you can move on to an even greater relationship, you must move past Mr. Ex and be openminded to Mr. Better.

There will be a time and a place to discuss the man who did you wrong, but not during the first few dates. When the subject is broached, it will speak volumes about your character if you don't throw him entirely under the bus by speaking of him in an unflattering light. This tells a man you keep it classy.

It is equally important to keep it to yourself if several years or months have passed since your last date. Leave it to a man's imagination that you have men lined up waiting around the corner. You don't want him to believe he is your only option or that you are starved for company. I'm not suggesting you lie – there is just no need to make full disclosure.

→ *Never Discuss the List.* You know the one. The list you've mentally made in your head a few times of the men you've slept with. Marriage material never-ever, in the history of ever, discloses the names or the number of men who are on *the list*. I'm not going to tell you what I believe to be a fair number because first, I don't judge, and secondly, you are never going to discuss the list with anyone. Including me. If a man presses you to answer, stand firm with military-like secrecy and reply, "I don't kiss and tell." There will always be times when you secretly wish there was a delete button that could be pushed when it comes to erasing the past of your sex life. If we just would have found out more about the person and showed more self-control. Don't beat yourself up. If you can't say, "I wish I wouldn't have done that," at least once, you haven't fully lived (or you may be a minor.)

→ *Don't Ever Have Sex with A Man on The First Date. Ever.* We've been taught this dating advice forever. For a man to view you *as* marriage material, you must be unique. And that means having standards. And having standards means you don't fall into bed on the first date. It's sad to say waiting to have sex makes you different, but in today's fast-paced internet dating society, where men only have to *swipe right* to get laid, it can be rare.

After Dates One, Two and Three

After the first goodnight kiss, there is nothing left to be done. Zilch, nada, absolutely nothing. No need to initiate contact by sending texts, emails, or Morse code after the first few dates. Don't make suggestions for future dates. The reason why is because now, more than ever, the ball is in his court. Doing otherwise leaves him with the impression you are working too hard to earn his love, affection, and attention.

Take it slow in the beginning. If Mr. Maybe calls or texts you right after a date to plan a second, great! Awesome! However, if he didn't follow-up with you immediately, understand that like you, he had a life before meeting you, which may keep him busy. Just as you, hopefully, have a busy life with work, family, friends, and a hobby that takes up your time, he probably has the same. In the beginning stages, there is absolutely no reason at all he should consider you a priority. Chances are he's swimming around in the dating pool just as you are. If you take it personally and lash out when he does take a week or two to call you with, "Where have you been?" and "Why haven't you called me?" In a bitchy way, he'll believe you to be insecure, too sensitive, and a bit too possessive.

Take the laid-back approach. Give it one to two weeks to play out and wait to see what happens next. Typically, an interested man will call within three days to a week. If he is super busy, two weeks' tops. If he hasn't called within two weeks, he didn't see a future with you right away. For now, he's decided not to bother pursuing you further. Oh well, no love loss. It was only a couple of dates. You shouldn't take it personally.

On the other hand, if and when he does call, respond with kindness, and act as if you didn't even notice the time lapse since your last date. Remember, the "hard to get" girl is super busy. Behaving in full bitch mode or showing your ass will not secure future dates. Think the old English proverb, "You catch more flies with honey than you do vinegar." Meaning: When he does call, he'll ask you out again if you remain sweet and kind. However, if you release the evil inner bitch who wants to know, "Why in the hell has it taken so long to call?" The odds of him asking you out again are slim to none.

Chapter 2

Why Independence is Your Key to Happiness

*"It is easy to be independent when you've got money.
But to be independent when you haven't got a thing,
that's the Lord's test."*

--Mahalia Jackson

Being independent conveys you're a no-BS kind of girl. It relays having a boyfriend is not what your entire universe revolves around. It sends the message you have a career you are passionate about, friends you enjoy spending time with, and having a fun, meaningful life of your own is at the forefront of your mind. You don't settle for less; you expect more.

A smart woman doesn't have a preconceived idea that he's the one after one little date. Instead, she is nonchalant. Picture a multimillion-dollar client, sitting in a large office in a New York City High Rise, letting an Advertisement Executive pitch his idea to her company.

An independent woman does not feel the need to make an official statement broadcasting her independence. If you must tell anyone of your independence, it reveals you have something to prove. He will be able to tell from the energy you put out. He'll know there is no hidden agenda, no ego, and more importantly, he will know you are where you *want* to be – not because you *need* to be.

When an independent woman meets an independent man, there is a certain vibe and energy they both put out. She is a huge turn on for a man due to his fear of waking up with a "Needy Nellie." Just as Spider-Man's 'spidey-sense' manifests in a tingling feeling at the base of his neck, alerting him to danger. A man can sense the energy from a needy woman, at which time he mentally rates her 1 through 5, according to the DEFCON Warning System. Mentally he begins to plan his escape. However, when a man feels as though you don't need him, his feet become anchored firmly in the ground as if he were standing in cement.

You will not hear an independent woman bitch about life or men taking advantage of her. She refuses to be the victim of life's circumstances. She has no expectation life will be perfect, but she views herself as a survivor and has a survivor mentality to back it up. She doesn't compromise when it comes to the basics, such as being valued, feeling heard, and feeling safe. She knows the way to challenge a man is with her mind, not her body. You also won't hear this woman cry wolf to gain attention or sympathy. She doesn't create drama to make her look like she is a helpless damsel in distress. Nor does she use tears for pity. She won't curl up in the fetal position when she is knocked down. Instead, she rises, adjusts her crown, and gets on with it.

She doesn't cancel her weekly Wednesday night out with the girls for drinks and dinner in hopes a new guy will want to take her out. She doesn't take matters into her own hands and make emotional attempts to contact him when he doesn't reach out to her. She knows if he doesn't call, it's his loss. She knows the most important thing a woman can have going on is her own thing. Whatever brings her happiness – she continues to do it.

She also won't transform who she is to appease somebody. She doesn't seek input on how to dress or act. She doesn't tolerate pressure from anyone. You won't hear her voice concern about what the opinions of people who are not close to her believe because she *doesn't care*. Those people do not enter her thoughts at all. She knows if someone is talking behind her back, she's two steps ahead of them.

When faced with a dilemma, she does her research to form an opinion and make informed decisions. This method articulates she can make her own choices. Once her mind is made up, she's not afraid to rock the boat sailing to her destination.

Do you remember when Destiny's Child released the single "*Independent Women?*" Women all over the world made "*I Depend on Me*" their motto. They proudly declared they had their own house, their own car, their own job, and were proudly living their own lives.

At one point, being viewed as an independent woman was misinterpreted to mean someone who did not *need* a man. We feared, to be independent, we would be regarded as a poster child for a movement that would cast us in an unfavorable light. In our society, we now know this does not hold true at all. An independent woman knows there is plenty of room in her life for love, only now women don't mind waiting longer to get it.

Why Being Independent Will Sky Rocket Your Confidence

Independent women naturally tend to be a little more confident in handling everyday issues. They know how valuable they are and want to make the right decisions to protect themselves. They are mentally prepared to act and do things instead of waiting for support or permission from others.

Being independent means, you will have the courage to try new things that intrigue you. It enables you to gain life experiences on your own. Women who rely on men for everything are inclined to believe they *need* a man in their life to breathe. Which makes a man feel too much pressure.

The frosting on the cake is retaining the ability to be independent, strong, soft, and feminine. Abandon the notion that being feminine makes you weak. *It makes you a woman.* And women are many things. There's nothing wrong with wearing the pants in the family -- *just add a touch of lace beneath.*

A Woman Who Is Driven, Has
Goals and A Plan in Place is a Huge Turn On

What's next in your life? Where are you headed? Men find women who have a plan in place and a passion for success ever so appealing. Why? Simply because a man worth a grain of salt also is driven, has goals, and a plan in place to pursue his own dreams and to make his own way. He wants someone who he can trust to support his dreams as well.

A lawyer asked a friend of mine out on a date several times before she finally agreed. Over dinner, he asked her, "Why did it take you so long to decide to go out with me?" It took him by surprise when she told him that on her off time, she invested in real estate and had been busy renovating a piece of property. He was taken by surprise that he'd been passed over for a housing project. He was impressed she had focus and passion for doing what she loved.

Men want an independent woman who knows what she wants and has a plan in action to pursue her vision. But don't confuse that to mean they want a second boss after they leave the office. After business hours, let your guard down and leave the take-charge attitude behind. On dates, expose your softer side.

Play Up Your Femininity

Don't confuse independence with masculinity, or masculinity with independence. At the end of the day, a man wants to be with a woman who is capable of being playful and compassionate. Femininity is an essential attribute that will keep him right by your side.

Men go weak at the knees for a woman who plays up her femininity. This is hard for the businesswoman who must have a take-charge attitude to comprehend fully. However, understand embracing your femininity will enhance every aspect of your life. Gloria Allred kicks ass in pink every single day, and Oprah hosted the highest-rated television talk show in stilettoes.

Play up your femininity by wearing feminine attire. If you wear black, navy, gray, and beige pantsuits with flats to work every day, dress it up by adding a blouse with a touch of color, jewelry, and high-heels. Switch it up by wearing dresses or a skirt. There's not a lady in the world who can't enhance her beauty with a touch of makeup and a dash of perfume. Oh, and never, ever leave home without a tube of lipstick.

Chapter 3

True Love Waits

"A lady's imagination is very rapid; it jumps from admiration to love, from love to matrimony in a moment."

-- Jane Austen

For some women, dating is fabulous. For others, it is like taking the final walk down death row before being placed on the execution table. Regardless of whether you love dating or dread it, most will agree once you find someone you are halfway compatible with, the anticipation of text messages, telephone calls, and then finally, the date is almost too much to bear.

Perhaps it's been weeks, months, or even years since you had a date. Now you have someone you are very interested in sitting across the table from you having drinks and dinner. You want Mr. Maybe to be Mr. Right. Before you begin to analyze, overthink, and start writing his last name with your first name to see if the two go together, whoa, back now. Take a deep breath and relax. From the start, set the right tone to demonstrate you have patience.

Many years ago, there was the '**K-I-S-S-I-N-G**' song used by kids on the playground or playing jump rope. It was sung by children to taunt or embarrass young kids who were in puppy love to make them feel uncomfortable.

> *Bobby and Amy*
> *sitting in a tree,*
> **Kay-Eye-Ess-Ess-Eye-En-Gee**
> *First comes love,*
> *then comes marriage,*
> *then comes baby in a baby carriage.*

Whoever wrote this catchy rhyme got it right. This timeline worked perfectly for our mothers, grandmothers, and great-grandmothers. Somehow, someway we screwed up the time frame and shuffled everything around. Now the baby comes first, marriage second, and in the end, we say a Hail Mary for love. Somewhere in the middle of the relationship, but often after the boudoir has been explored, is when women perk up and attempt to find out exactly who the hell she's sleeping with and what his intentions are.

Once you have sex, the powerful hormone oxytocin, also known as the cuddle hormone, is flooding through your body. Now you believe you are hopelessly in love. *NOW* you've decided you want more, and it is at this time you decide you want to investigate and interrogate to find out if Mr. Maybe shares the qualities, values, and beliefs you want in Mr. Right. *I'm not judging; we've all been there, done that.* Eventually, when one discovers they don't share the same dreams, their feelings ultimately become hurt when said relationship does not measure up, or he doesn't reciprocate with the same lovey-dovey feelings you have. You wanted the whole kit and caboodle, and he only wanted a one-night fling. *Ouch.* That hurts!

The best strategy while dating in the beginning stages is to ask questions over some time. Not an outright interrogation, but ask questions about his life, job, long-term goals, friends, and family. During this time, gather enough information to find out if he is going to make room in his life for you.

On the First Few Dates Avoid Discussing...

- Your plans for marriage.
- You want a big family.
- You want *his* financial support.
- You're past bad breakups.
- You don't waste your time on men without a plan.
- Your dating rules.
- The name of your therapist.
- How much debt you're in.
- Sex talk; and
- What self-help books you're reading.

Instead, make him the limelight of the night. Men love to talk about many topics, but his favorite subject of choice is himself. Think about the lyrics to Toby Keith's hit song *"I Wanna Talk About Me."*

I want to talk about me

Want to talk about I
Want to talk about number one
Oh my me my
What I think, what I like, what I know, what I want, what I see
I like talking about you, you, you, you usually, but occasionally
I want to talk about me

You get the idea. Before you allow yourself to become emotionally attached, make a point to know the answers to your questions before you give the ultimate prize -- *your love, yourself, your body*. Be like a secret service agent, always on a mission to guard and protect your heart. Investigate in a stealth-like manner to gather top-secret intelligence to determine if he is the right one for you. More times than not, the alarm bells will go off and alert you to the fact you are not compatible, which will save lots of time and heartache in the long run. If you are the type of woman who jumps in with both feet before knowing how hot the water is, now is an excellent time to adjust your dating strategy before you get burned.

Also, after the first date, avoid being the first to reveal your feelings like how much you truly like him, enjoy his company, or how you "haven't had this much fun on a date in years." Don't ask, "If I give you my heart, will you promise never to break it?" Allow him time to divulge his feelings for you first, and then if you feel the same, tell him.

Let him be the one who suggests dates. Don't drop hints by asking what his plans are for upcoming weekends or holidays. Thank him for dinner *before* he leaves for the night. Don't send a text or make a phone call to thank him for dinner after the fact.

This cries out, "eager."

Diving into the relationship pool too fast will often leave you in water with sharks. Demonstrating patience during the first few months to get to know a man will help you avoid an unwelcome relationship you will later regret, or the worst, at the local police station filing for a restraining order. Establishing patience in the beginning also demonstrates you are a woman who has control.

You can avoid rushing into relationships by simply getting to know a man first. Make a promise to yourself; you won't become emotionally vested in the initial phase of dating. Just get to know him and allow him the pleasure of knowing you. If you want the commitment of marriage, you have a motive. You want the ring, the flowers, the gown, the fairy tale wedding, and of course, the groom. You want the three-bedroom, two-bath house you make a home. You want the SUV you'll one day chauffeur your kids to baseball games and dance recitals. Before you get the benefits that come along with marriage, you must focus on discovering what the potential Mr. Right is looking for in a woman. If he wants a no strings attached, friends with benefits kind of fling, you should move on immediately and have the *"Thank you very much for not wasting my sweet time,"* mentality. Unless, of course, you only want a no strings attached, friends with benefits kind of fling.

First, determine if you both are even well-suited. After a few dates, you may decide you have a personality conflict. He may be rude to waitresses, and who in the hell can date a man who is offensive to the waitstaff? If you take time, in the beginning, to find out this crucial information, you reduce the chances of wasting your precious time in the future.

Men and women alike want a combination of things. *Love, romance, sex, companionship.* Just not always at the same time, or in the same order. You have to decide on your own which ones are the most important to him, at the current time, if any at all, before you try to woo him with the goods.

People who have successful marriages will tell you trust is the superglue that holds relationships together. If you have a longtime best friend, I bet a mutual trust and respect exists. Best friends have a certain openness. You can trust a bestie with your carefully guarded secrets with little to no fear of being judged for who you are. While dating, trust is earned over time because there is an unknown territory each is exploring.

Chapter 4

Full Disclosure

"Sex is hardly ever just about sex."
--Shirley MacLaine

Steve Martin once said, "Don't have sex, man. It leads to kissing, and pretty soon, you have to start talking to them." Some women may argue we are no longer living in a society where men and women don't have double standards. But yes ma'am, yes, we still do. If you believe it doesn't matter to a man how long you wait before sleeping with him, think again.

What to Do When a Man Discloses He Is Not Looking For A Serious Commitment

Sometimes a man will be completely upfront and tell you he doesn't want a girlfriend or that he doesn't have the time to commit himself to an exclusive relationship. When a man discloses he is "Not looking for a serious relationship right now," for fuck's sake, believe what he is telling you. Respond with the sweetest smile, thank him for his honesty, and place him on your "friend" list. Don't stick around to try to change his mind. Don't try to cast a magic love spell for him to feel your love. Move on.

If you do try to change his mind, the day will come when you will want more and will eventually ask, *"Where is this going?"* He will kindly remind you of the night he disclosed to you the fact he did not want a serious relationship as if he did you a service. If he could miraculously produce a court reporter out of thin air to read from the transcript the exact language he used during the conversation, he would happily do so.

In the movie *"A Beautiful Mind,"* Russell Crowe portrayed John Nash, a brilliant man who struggled with paranoid schizophrenia. In one scene, Crowe's character says to his girlfriend, Alicia. "I find you very attractive. Your aggressive moves toward me indicate that you feel the same way. But still, ritual requires that we go through a number of platonic activities before we [brief pause] have sex. I'm simply proceeding with those activities. But in point of actual fact, all I really want to do is have intercourse with you as soon as possible."

A man knows that if he were to approach you with, "Hi, I just want to fuck you," his time would be better spent searching for unicorns, the pot of gold at the end of the rainbow, or the needle in the haystack. He believes if he sugar coats it, a woman will believe she can change his mind with her secret powers and convince him a relationship is just what he wanted. In the meantime, he's getting everything he wants from you, but giving nothing in return.

Men have always categorized women into two groups. The

fun time girl, we'll call the *lollipop,* a piece of candy who sits on a stick and gives it away, 'it' meaning sex. She believes the only way to keep a man's attention is by offering sex to satisfy his sexual needs. Or, the second category, *Marriage Material,* also known as *"the one."* She is the girl a man will bend down on one knee to ask the question that consists of the four little words you are sitting on pins and needles to hear, "Will you marry me?" She is the woman he brought home to meet mom and pop. She is the woman who has principles, is the woman who can hold a conversation, and she is the one he parades around his family, friends, and co-workers. She is the woman who possesses:

- ✓ Confidence
- ✓ Honesty
- ✓ Emotional Stability
- ✓ Patience
- ✓ Strength
- ✓ Independence
- ✓ Security

It is possible after one night of heated bliss a man will propose to you. There have been many marriages (and divorces) that followed after going to bed with a man on the first date. There is also one in two hundred and ninety-two million chances of you winning the Powerball Jackpot. This advice is for the two hundred and ninety-two million women who don't win the lottery in the love department after having sex on the first date.

Physical attraction will only get you so far. To be the last woman standing, you must connect on an emotional and intellectual level as well. You must maintain your power, and you keep your power by not using sex as your only high card. Sex doesn't seal the deal.

Having sex too soon will make a man happy for a few hours. But, he'll think it's nothing special because he got it too soon. If you view sex as standard and ordinary as you do brushing your teeth, he will treat you as standard and average and discard you without a thought. He'll assume you go to bed with every man on the first date.

Imagine a night out with your best girlfriend, who you've met at your favorite bar. You see a handsome man having a drink with a few of his friends. Your eyes meet, lock for a few seconds, and bang! You've just had your first moment with this man.

Later that evening, he sends cocktails over for you and your friends and then slowly makes his way over to your table. You spend the next two hours having a great conversation and then move to the dance floor where things get slow and sweet.

Stop.

If you were to end the night right here, where things got "slow and sweet" and sent him on his merry way, he would leave the bar thinking of ways to see you again. He would wonder what it would take to see you another time and wonder what he would have to do to win you over. He would probably find time to track you down the next day to make plans for a future date. But if it goes from "slow and sweet" to "hot and heavy," and a goodnight kiss turned into a night where you are staring at the ceiling wondering, "who is this man?" It's likely, the next day, he will be busy in meetings.

When he leaves, which is before you have time to fall asleep, he reflects the eight-dollar drink he purchased was an excellent investment. It had a high return, which paid off quickly. Meanwhile, as you try to fall asleep, you question if he is ever going to call again? You can eliminate this question from your life altogether if you understand that making him wait for sex is not for your benefit, it's for *his*. To increase your chances of him cuddling with you through the night instead of hitting the road after the *Big O*, slow down a bit and let him chase you. After you give him all there is to give, he has no desire to go out of his way.

A "lollipop" believes just because a man loves sex, all she must do is give the man sex, and then poof! The man magically falls in love with her, right? *Wrong!* A woman who is dating for keeps knows sex is not an invitation, nor is it a guarantee of a monogamous relationship. A man will boast to his friends about the girl who invited him over to "Netflix and chill." He knows you will say, "I didn't plan on having sex with you," "I promise I've never done that before." and then he laughs afterward. You are now nothing more than a punch line.

The Million Dollar Question

The million-dollar question has always been, "How long do I wait before having sex?" Some experts believe every woman should stick to the three-date rule. You know, no sex until the third date. Others believe it is best to wait three months. Yes... that's right, ninety days. The debate on when to have sex has gone on for centuries, and we still don't have a sure-fire, concrete, solid answer. A century ago, if a young woman had sex before marriage, she was considered a 'ruined' woman. Now women want to know, "Why they can't have sex with whoever they want,

LESLIE BRASWELL

whenever they want?"

If you have sex on the first date, chances are he'll consider it a deal-breaker. Of course, he wants sex as all men do. But if you do the deed on the first date, he'll believe you have no restraint, no willpower, no self-control, and no self-respect.

Another problem with having sex too soon is knowing where to take the relationship from there. You have shared a very private, intimate moment quickly. Does that mean the rest of the relationship moves quickly? Are you now considered a couple? If not, will your feelings be hurt?

If you have been friends for a long time and then sleep with him on a first date, it could turn into something extraordinary. And I'm rooting for you as I believe the best romances are between two people who start out as friends.

If you make a man wait too long for sex, he may feel you are using sex to control the outcome of the relationship. Some say it's simply impractical to think you can date someone for three to four months without having sex. The longer you can hold off, the better your chances are. What's important is to let him know you want to take the time to know him better. A quality man will be understanding. If he is *not* understanding of you wanting to wait, cut his ass loose immediately.

While there may be no correct answer because each person and every situation is different. *It's all arguable.* What has been proven time and time again are women who put off sex for as long as they possibly can, have the 2.5 karat ring, and the man who adores her. This proves the old-fashioned notion -- true love does, in fact, wait.

What to Do When You Have Gone
To Bed with A Man Too Soon?

If you have slipped and fallen in-between the sheets too soon, he may have already formed a conclusion about you and labeled you the lollipop girl. This blunder is nearly impossible to fix. He will not view you as wife material unless you can persuade him he's the exception, and you really, honestly, don't ever go to bed with a man so early on. To fix this slip-up, you must slow down and make him see the sweet, charming qualities you possess. This isn't an easy mission to accomplish. As a matter of fact, it's near impossible, as it is much simpler to make him see you as marriage material *before* you give it up than after.

Whether you intended to or not, the dynamics of the relationship just went up a level. Now you're being watched like a hawk to see if you are moving towards monogamy. Before sleeping with a quality man, you must build upon attraction first. I say this because men are visual beings. Beauty is only blind to a blind man. There aren't many men who would kick you out of bed. There are a lot of beautiful, successful (*clingy*) single women out in the world.

The beginning stages are when the future of your relationship is mapped out. When you sleep with a man early on, it is more probable than not; he will only view you as a 'friends with benefits' type of girl. Not the woman he will take home to meet his parents. He will never get to know the woman who possesses the sweet qualities that make you, you.

Without creating attraction first, the committed relationship will be hard to develop because you have already revealed to him every single one of your high cards. There is nothing left in your bag of tricks. If you had given him the grand prize before he had to compete, there is nothing more for him to look forward to. You've given up your power. Think of how a professional football player would perform if he were given the bonus paycheck, the trophy and the big diamond super bowl ring at the beginning of the season. What incentive would he have to compete and perform, week after week, if he was given everything upfront?

Most contract lawyers will advise you once both parties have signed a contract, you cannot change the terms of the contract unless agreed to by both sides. The same can hold true for having sex too soon. For some, sex is a part of love, and for others, love is not a part of sex. To have the love you want along with great sex, a mutual attraction must exist before the sex begins. Once Pandora's Box has been opened, you just can't close the box again; you can't change from having sex to not having sex without feelings being hurt. What you can do is be honest and say, "I want to slow down. I feel we are taking this too fast. Hopefully, he'll respect you for being upfront.

Three Emotions One Should Never Feel After Sex

➢ *Regret* for sleeping with a man too soon;
➢ *Fear* a man will leave you if you don't have sex; and
➢ *The pressure* to sleep with a man.

If he makes his exit because you have not had sex at the beginning of a relationship, then thank your lucky stars he got away. Your goal is to find passion and happiness in the love department. Regret and feelings of guilt or remorse, because you did not live up to his expectations, should never weigh heavily on your mind.

What you should do is arm yourself with knowledge of the male mind. Always want and expect to receive what is best for you as a woman. Make no mistake; men still want to have sex and always, always will. However, what they need to feel to fall in love is a deep emotional *attraction*. A man will not come right out and tell you that bit of advice because he places sex before love. He'll be happy as a dog with a bone with 'just sex' if you expect nothing more.

More Than Just a Vagina

Some women believe the only thing they have to offer is one of a sexual nature. Ultimately, when the relationship fails to flourish, the feeling of disappointment and despair enters their mind. The self-esteem level some women possess is so low; they just do not know what else to offer. So, she gives the one part of herself she knows a man wants. *Sex.*

When the man does not call or make plans to see her again, she's left feeling used, hurt and unloved. To make a man value you, value yourself. Understand you bring more to a relationship than just a vagina.

The best relationships are where both people receive and give love, which is equally beneficial to one another. Before you give your body, make sure you are positively receiving everything you want from the relationship. It's just like paying to have your yard mowed. You don't hand over the payment before the grass has been cut. You wait until the lawn is manicured to perfection and done according to your standards. Only then do you hand over the cash.

Allow a man to have plenty of time to see how irresistibly attractive, fun, and fascinating you are. Prove to be an asset to him. Give him time to become more interested in committing himself to you. Show him you are more than a one-night stand. Let the tension build up slowly so it will be a better experience for both of you. You'll know when the timing is right.

Chapter 5

Stay Ready, so you don't have to Get Ready

"I say luck is when an opportunity comes along, and you're prepared for it."

— Denzel Washington

The Girl Scout motto: *Be Prepared.* A confident woman stays ready, so she doesn't have to spend the day to get ready. She doesn't have to spend all day having her hair done, makeup applied, and a last-minute manicure and pedicure for a Saturday night date. She doesn't go for the homeless look during the week just to shine up like a new penny at the last minute.

There are a few things every woman needs to keep her confidence level sky high and date ready always. Your daily presence will always influence your confidence level, so splurge and invest in your appearance. If your hair and makeup look good, it increases your confidence level. If you can't afford to treat yourself to the basics, you can learn to do them yourself at home with no problem.

Wearing a little amount of makeup to show you care about your appearance is excellent. It tells a man you want to look your best while with him and for him. Wearing too much conveys you're trying too hard. Don't be afraid to go all-natural now and then. A woman who is comfortable and confident enough to wear none is far better than wearing too much.

Many women speak with their hands using gestures and motions. Men find manicured hands and nails to be feminine. No need to wait until date night to have your nails done. Stay *It-girl* ready and have them professionally done at least every three weeks. If your polish is chipping or cracking, take it entirely off. Don't leave the house with chipped nail polish; it should be all there or nothing at all.

Men absolutely notice manicured feet. Some have a foot fetish. Schedule a pedicure every two to three weeks, even in the winter. If having a pedicure is not in your budget, learn how to give one to yourself. When all of you looks good, all of you feels good.

You may remember the movie *Boomerang. The film stars* Eddie Murphy, who portrays Marcus Graham, the smart, high-powered ad exec with a sexy arrogance.

Marcus was a perfectionist when it came to women, from their pretty heads all the way down to their toes. He didn't seem to have a foot fetish, but after sleeping with a woman after a date, he discovered her corn-covered toes, and carefully slipped right out of the sheets.

You should never have to go shopping on the day of a date to find something to wear that night. By the time your date picks you up, you'll be exhausted. Your clothes should fit like a glove to avoid tugging, fidgeting, and adjusting, which makes women appear uncomfortable. Nancy, a friend of mine who owns a high-end dress shop, gave me the following excellent advice. To eliminate the pre-date nervous butterflies, you should have three things in your closet always.

✓   The classic LBD (Little Black Dress) to cover the three C's - Church, cocktails, or cemeteries. In the fashion world, the LBD is considered a vital piece of your wardrobe. A simple LBD can be dressed up or down, depending on the circumstances. For instance, add a jacket and Mary-Jane heels to wear to the office. Do you have to attend a funeral? Black is the official color of mourning. It's also the signature look of sophistication. For cocktails and dinner, add jewelry and pretty accessories.

✓   Jeans and a beautiful blouse are textbook if you are going out for a night on the town or staying at home. Find the perfect pair of jeans that fit like a glove and have them washed, ready, and waiting in your closet.

✓   A Designer handbag just because a great purse makes everything else you are wearing look better. You can't go wrong with one neutral in color that can be combined with anything in your closet.

Chances are slim to none a man knows what designer clothing you may or may not be wearing. Men could care less whether you buy your clothes at Saks or off the rack. What they do pay attention to is that you are dressed appropriately for the occasion. Invited to a golf tournament? Leave the stilettos in the closet. Have dinner reservations at a classy restaurant? Don't go with the slutty or the homeless look. On days where you don't have time to get fully dressed, remember sunglasses and a ball cap are like fresh paint. They hide a multitude of sins.

In his book "Act Like a Lady, Think Like a Man," Steve Harvey wrote, "One of the biggest misconceptions that a woman has is that a man has to accept her the way she is. No, we don't. I don't know who told you that. We like the bright and shiny. If you stop wearing the makeup, stop putting on nail polish, stop wearing high heels, you'll lose us." The more you act like a feminine lady, a prize, a catch, the more he will treat you as such.

Remember, putting forth a little effort in your appearance flatters a man, and it makes you feel one thousand times more confident. When he walks into a room with you holding on to his arm, he wants heads to turn in your direction. Why? Because having a woman who is a little bit out of his league, holding his hand, inflates his ego to the size of a hot air balloon. He wants to be proud of the woman he's standing by. Take Blake Shelton's recent Tweet about girlfriend Gwen Stefani, "I feel like the fat, ugly guy in high school that got the hottest girl to go to the prom with him." Sigh.

Always Keep Your House Date Night Ready

Regardless of whether you live in a mansion on a hill, a neighborhood in the suburbs, a small New York City apartment, or a trailer home on a country road, your home should be reflective of who you are. When you do finally invite a man over, chances are he will judge you based on not what you live in or where, but how well you keep your home. I make this point because not only do you need to keep yourself ready for a date, you need to keep your home ready as well.

Your home should make anyone who enters feel comfortable and welcome. Walkthrough your home and take note as to what you need to do to make it date night ready, and get it done. Having a clean house costs nothing more than your time. If cleaning isn't your thing, hire a service to do it for you. A messy home is a huge turn off to a man.

When selling a home, the first suggestion a real estate agent makes is to declutter each room. This will make a huge difference and is entirely free. Make sure everything has a place and is in its place. Clothes belong in the closets along with your shoes. If your clothes are scattered throughout your house, pick them up and hang them in a closet. If dirty clothes are strewn about your home, at least put them in the clothes hamper if you don't have time to do laundry. If your laundry room has clothes piled high like pyramids to the ceiling, close the door.

- ✓ Are dishes piled high in the kitchen? Take time to wash and put away.
- ✓ Trash stinks. Take it out.
- ✓ If you have a mountain of bills stacked on your desk, hide them.
- ✓ Remove any pictures of past boyfriends.
- ✓ In the bathroom, hide all feminine products, medications, yeast infection creams and hide under lock and key any unopened pregnancy tests.
- ✓ Hide this book along with other self-help titles.

Make the absolute best of what you have. Taking time to get your home organized makes you feel so much better. And it reveals to a man you have your life together. When you do invite Mr. Maybe over, you'll feel so put together.

Chapter 6

The Gift of Mystery

"There's nothing more powerful than a woman who knows how to contain her power and not let it leak, standing firmly within it in mystery and silence. A woman who talks too much sheds her allure."

-- Marianne Williamson

In today's world, reality television and social media leave little to the imagination. Being a little enigmatic gives a woman an air of secrecy and excitement. Mark Twain once wrote, "There is a charm about the forbidden that makes it unspeakably desirable." Remaining a bit mysterious and a little private makes a man want to know more about you.

If you have been living each waking moment of your life through social media, retaining a touch of mystery may not be a bad idea. Sometimes the less you reveal, the more attractive you become. To become a little mysterious, don't talk excessively or provide *too* much information. Being just a little bit private captivates a man's interest and keeps it. Instead of rambling on and on about your life, ask more questions, providing little information about yourself.

A man will not grow tired of a mystery woman because she never wears out her welcome. She doesn't attend every social event because she has no fear of missing out. Instead, she makes a man guess if she will attend or not. When she is a "no show," she does not offer an explanation.

A clingy woman will stick around until the busboys come out to clear off the tables. Staying too long leaves the impression she has nowhere to go and nothing better to do. On the flip side, a man will never have to show a confident woman the door because she always knows when to leave. Leaving first leaves a man guessing what you are doing, where you're going, and who you are with.

A clingy woman responds to text messages within eighteen seconds, even while she is at work. Her smartphone is practically attached to her hand. She may break a collarbone trying to answer her phone, if, by chance, it's out of reach.

The confident woman does not live with her smartphone in her hand and doesn't always respond to text messages immediately. But she does respond timely if a response is warranted. She has no problem letting phone calls go straight to voicemail if she is working, visiting with friends, or on a date. She returns phone calls and text messages when it's convenient for her to respond.

A Mysterious Woman Doesn't Provide an Itinerary

A clingy woman wants a man to know how to contact her just in case *he* decides he would like to make plans to see her. She may take the liberty of entering her work, cell number, and email address on his phone herself. The minute she can, she sends a friend request on Facebook, follows him on Twitter, and does a quick search to see what other social media outlets they share. She does all this the first day she meets him before he leaves her sight. Not a woman who is hard to get. He'll have to chase her through the parking lot to get her contact information.

A clingy woman may sit and wait (phone in hand) for a man to ask her out, even if it means she's left alone, without plans on a Friday or Saturday night. Not a confident woman –she plans weekends away with her friends, family, or doesn't mind going out alone. She doesn't always provide him with details about her whereabouts, which gives him the impression she has people to meet and places to be. She doesn't keep her schedule free and clear in hopes she'll be asked out at the last minute. She doesn't stay cooped indoors, waiting for a last-minute phone call. Instead, she gets out and enjoys a beautiful day.

Before You Push The Friend or Follow Button

One great way to keep a touch of mystery is to become a little more private on social media sites. Foremost, I recommend keeping your settings set to private for safety purposes because why on earth would you not? And understand what you put on social media is just as important as the first impression you make.

Do you Friend or Follow each man you meet? A smart

rule to follow is to let the man send you a request first. Just because of all the new technology available doesn't mean you shouldn't still follow Grandma's advice, "don't seek him out," and "let him come to you." Also, wait longer than thirty seconds before you accept a friend request if you are interested in a serious long-term relationship. Ask yourself if you want the stress of knowing who the other five hundred and eighty-two other women he's friends with on social media? And who in the hell is that cute girl who liked his status? Even if you're not the jealous type, you may be the *curious* type and feel the need to do a little internet research.

We've learned men love the hunt. They love the chase. It's the thrill of the chase men want and crave. So, let him be the hunter and do his own research. By putting all your information out for him to read like a book, you're not allowing a man to be the hunter. If you have a GPS attached to your hand and you post or tweet your entire daily routine, he won't find the need to call you to know how your day is going and what you are doing. Give him a reason to call you.

It's hard to remain mysterious when you post your every move for the world to see. If you don't wait until a man has taken the time to get to know you, you deprive him of the chase. All one needs to do is look at your "about me" page to learn:

- Where you work.
- Where you went to school.
- Where you live.
- Where you are from.
- Who your family is.
- Your birthday.

- Your religion.
- Your political views.
- Your favorite bands.
- Your favorite television shows.
- Your favorite books; and
- Your favorite activities.

It's too much information, too soon! With your entire life history available at his fingertips, no conversation is necessary. There is no mystery about you anymore. Some women treat their Facebook and Twitter pages like a scrapbook. If he knows you went to California last year and has seen all the fabulous pictures of you skydiving, there is simply no need to tell him about it. He already knows.

You may believe being friends on social media sites is a harmless gesture, but men aren't seduced down the aisle because of a woman's fascinating status updates. One woman posted continuously on her boyfriend's Facebook wall, "You make me so happy," and "I'm so lucky to have you in my life." Which seems harmless enough, but what does it say when he doesn't take the time to hit the like button? An interested man may post sweet nothings on your wall to make you happy, but wouldn't it make you more thrilled to hear those sweet nothings in person?

Women believe simple, harmless little posts don't make a difference, but what you put in cyberspace speaks volumes about your character. Posting on social media sites should reflect the fantastic, smart, fascinating woman you are. Never make a post which makes you appear to be promiscuous, or less than favorable. Refrain from posting provocative pictures, guzzling your favorite tequila, or sending last-minute invitations to all your male friends. It screams desperation!

A Few Social Media Do's and Don'ts
(Warning: There are more Don'ts than Do's)

- Don't be the first to Friend, Follow, Wink, Poke, or Swipe right.
- Don't be the first to post photos of the two of you.
- Don't ask to take selfies with him on the first date.
- Don't tag him in photos.
- Don't check him into places.
- Don't be the first to change your relationship status.
- Don't like each one of his status updates. (One 'Like' for every three to four posts.)
- Don't friend or follow his friends or family.
- Don't private message his friends or family.
- Don't send private messages or chats to him; let him send them to you, first. Remember, let him take the lead.
- Don't comment on photos, unless he has mentioned you.
- Don't post sixty-seven status updates a day describing every single detail of your day.
- Don't post rants about dating disasters.
- Don't break into his social media account.

Instead...

- Do accept his Friend request *after a few hours.*
- Like some of his photos.
- Sporadically post pictures that depict your fun-filled life. If you just took a trip to your favorite beach, perfect. A night out with friends, even better. Post away.

Women who have a strong sense of self don't feel the need to post each event in their life to feel important or prove how great a life they live. The smartest way to leave a man hungry for more is by giving him less to work with. Create your interests, your hobbies, die-hard work ethics, and anything which you believe defines you and let that be how you present yourself to the world. Just keep it real and make your social media reflective of the super fabulous soul you are. Remember, how you present yourself to the world is precisely how the world will perceive you.

When it comes to communicating by way of texts, IMs, or any other form, it's imperative you set the tone from the beginning. Men and women alike are guilty of creating entire relationships via their electronic device of choice. But we fall in love through communicating face to face, through touch, and hearing the other laugh. Obviously, you had to communicate to make a date, but it wouldn't hurt him to think you don't live with your smartphone bonded to your hand.

You accomplish this on the first date, or whenever you are with him, by turning your phone on silent. Not on vibrate, but on complete silence. First, this gives him your undivided attention, which a man deserves while on a date. Secondly, when you are apart from him and don't respond to his texts immediately, he'll wonder what you're doing.

You can also casually mention you turn your phone on silent after ten o'clock p.m., so your sleep isn't interrupted by friends' texting late at night. This also prevents midnight calls and hopefully will result in him contacting you sooner by calling to hear your sweet voice.

A Smart Woman Doesn't Put All of Her Eggs in One Basket

Too often, after a few dates, a woman will fall under the false assumption she is exclusively dating one man. She falls in love too quickly; meanwhile, he has her and several other women on his rotation list. While she is waiting on commitment night after lonely night, providing her loyalty, he's swimming around in the dating pool. She is left heartbroken, time after time.

Where women often fail is by devoting all their time and attention to one man who has her on a rotation. Not the "It Girl," this woman continues to accept dates from multiple men when asked. She gets out and meets people. She is aware finding love means getting out and about and meeting as many men as possible. She understands the power of choice and keeping her options open is crucial to getting what she wants.

She keeps a man on his toes by ever so delicately making him aware she has men on the back burner ready, willing, and able to take his place. Think like Mae West, "Ten men waiting for me at the door? Send one of them home, I'm tired," she once said. Unless you are in a long-term committed relationship, you should be dating several men. Until he broaches the subject of monogamy, you should continue to have lunch, drinks, and dinner plans with as many dates as your schedule will allow. Have a full life.

A good rule to follow is not to let a man know you really like him right off the bat unless he tells you first. Leave him wanting more by never allowing him to believe he has you completely figured out, which keeps him on his toes. When a man gets lazy in the relationship, you can gently get his attention by putting a little bit of mystery back into the picture. A simple, effective way to accomplish this is by being unreachable. If you can't resist the urge to respond to text messages within sixteen seconds, turn your phone to silent and put it away for a few hours each day to avoid the temptation to be so readily available.

Don't Feel Guilty Dating Multiple men

If a man is interested in you, he will be planning dates well in advance. If he's not making plans to see you and another man invites you on a date in the meantime, you should go, guilt-free. Just because one has paid for a few meals doesn't mean you have been purchased for the night, week, or month. A smart woman knows a forty-dollar filet mignon buys nothing.

What you can *assume* is when a man is not making plans with you consistently, you are not a priority for him. Even in today's fast-paced dating scene, he should have the courtesy to give you notice. And men usually have no problems making plans because the last thing he wants is to be left with his penis in his hand on a Friday or Saturday night.

The Benefits of Dating Several Men

• Emotional Freedom – You won't be emotionally dependent on one man.
• A Backup Plan. – If one-man cancels, another takes his place.
• Options - One man for every night of the week.
• Plans - An event that prevents you from being overly available and keeps you busy, so you don't over-analyze.

Date Other Men for Good, Not Evil

Using jealousy to make a man pursue you will ultimately always fail. He'll feel like he's not a priority to you, which will cause his ego to deflate to the size of a matchbox. So, while it's perfectly acceptable dating multiple men because you *want* to keep your options open, dating other men to make another feel jealous is a form of manipulation that should never be used. And would you really want to take the chance of losing a standup guy who couldn't recover from the thought of you with another man?

Chapter 7

Charm and Disarm Your Way into His Heart

"A good woman is one who loves passionately, has guts, seriousness, and passionate convictions takes responsibility, and shapes society."

— *Betty Friedan*

Foolish women *play* hard to get. Real women *are* hard to get. The difference between the two is one is pretending to be someone you're not. It takes a lot of effort to pretend to be anything other than your authentic self. It involves planning, scheming, and manipulation to get a man to chase you. None of which will work in the long run. Everyone's true colors eventually come out. When you are a woman, who is hard to get, you are far too busy creating a great life, working your hardest to make each day the best; you barely notice when a man has his sights set on you. Men can sense when a woman is *not* genuine, and this is precisely the behavior that will keep him on a quest for another woman.

Adopt the mindset a man is more like a bonus that enhances your life, which is already the most remarkable life ever. When you start dating someone new, don't forget about your friends, hobbies, and everything you did before meeting him. Remain focused on work and your social life. Continually strive to better yourself. A man becomes captivated by a woman who is authentically happy, self-assured, and confident simply because he knows she won't depend on him for her happiness.

A Sense of Humor Seals the Deal

One of the main characteristics' women love in a man is a good sense of humor. I'll confess, it's why I fell in love with my husband. He makes me laugh every single day. Men love to laugh just as much as women. They find one who doesn't take herself too seriously, very attractive. A man wants to know a woman isn't too uptight. However, don't confuse funny with silly. Silly women are just, well, *silly*. They usually end up on the "friends" list.

If you learn to laugh at yourself and turn your embarrassing moments into great stories to tell, others will find them amusing. A man will laugh with you and have a memorable time in the process. If you can laugh at yourself and others, it shows him you know how to have fun.

If you don't consider yourself funny, try to learn a new joke every week and always have a personal story saved for a night out. Watch anything with Tina Fey or Amy Schumer. You need not be born with a sense of humor. Some attributes are acquired.

Fashionable, not Superficial

Ultimately men care more about how a woman is put

together. Attire is secondary to a great personality and confidence. Most men could not identify one designer purse from another and could care less. They're imagining whatever you're wearing, torn off you, thrown on the floor.

Men understand Kim Kardashian West probably has the best wardrobe in existence. However, he would be horrified if you dressed like her on a date, and he wouldn't invite you over to meet his parents. They know she's just too high maintenance.

Use clothes to enhance your beauty, not detract from it. How you dress plays a huge factor when you first meet a man because it forms his first impression, which takes only seconds to create, even if it is an incorrect one.

He wants to know you can clean up shiny as a new diamond, but also be able to get down and dirty with the best of them. Take Carol Lombard, Clark Gable's late wife. It has been reported she loved to attend parties in low-cut, silk dresses, but would also go on duck hunts with him dressed like what some people described as a ragamuffin. He was crazy for her. Mix a little bit of modesty with a dash of sensuality; then, you may have found the golden ticket.

Have an Interest Which Does Not Require a Man's Participation

They want to know your happiness does not depend on them spending twenty-four hours, seven days a week entertaining you. Perhaps you're a working mom who's trying to balance a full-time job, raise happy kids, and take care of a home. A hobby may be the last thing on your mind. But you must have a life, or your own thing to do that makes you happy. Everyday living, work, relationships, and family can consume your time and leave you too tired for hobbies for yourself. Finding balance can be hard, but it's the most important thing you can do for yourself.

Many women are not passionate about anything. Some barely have time to shave their legs, much less have a chance to dedicate themselves to be enthusiastic about anything. Suddenly a man walks into their lives, and he becomes their *only* interest. A woman may spend every waking hour of her day being so *passionate* about her new man, it looks more pathetic.

Avoid this scenario at all costs by having an identity outside of work, being a mom and girlfriend. Taking the time to make yourself a priority is just the best thing you will ever do for yourself. What is it that would make your life a content one? What you were passionate about in your twenties may not hold your interest in your thirties, forties, or fifties. You may have to find a whole new interest. Seek, and you shall find.

Each one of us has a desire to provide value in not only our life but the lives of the people we are around each day. You must discover what your passion is that makes you matter, feel important, and gives you an identity of your own.

Men need "me time" also. Many men had hobbies before their relationship began only to have their significant others criticize the amount of time he devotes to his favorite pastime of choice. After the relationship is underway, some women become resentful about the time he spends on his interests.

If you are truly comfortable in your skin, you'll be accepting of the time he devotes to his hobby. One man told me he had made plans to visit his parents for the weekend. His girlfriend made plans to go hiking and posted to Facebook pictures of her along with her best friends hiking up a mountain having a great time. The fact was he did not have to worry about her while he was gone, which in his eyes made her more attractive.

Don't Lecture or Give the Third Degree

Lectures are better suited for college professors to their students. Men don't want to be lectured about what they should or should not do. If you become a constant nag, you will eventually notice his gaze dart upward at the ceiling, check the time on his watch or look off in the distance. He doesn't hear a word you say because he has tuned you out. Mentally, he's planning his escape route.

The woman who listens demonstrates she cares and is interested. Not offering your advice unless it is asked for reveals you have the virtue of patience. So many alpha males have the need to work through problems on their own before they feel comfortable talking about them with you. Sometimes it's better to sit back and listen before you offer your problem-solving advice.

If You Are Under The Impression
Men Are Turned Off By Women
With Ambition, Think Again

Men are not turned off by a woman who has drive, determination, and who loves her career. It demonstrates to them you have a "get-up-and-go" mindset. What men have repeatedly said is they are completely turned off by masculine energy. They want authenticity, genuine caring, kindness, and an easy-going approach. They want a woman who can engage them in conversation, challenge them to become a better man and captivate their attention. If you can mix brainpower together with femininity, you may possess the Midas touch.

Let Him Treat You Like a Lady --

- Let him be a gentleman to you.
- Let him open doors for you.
- Let him pick you up for dates.
- Let him spoil you.
- Let him take care of you.
- Dress up for him in feminine clothes.
- Let him plan the date and make reservations.
- Agree to disagree. Don't always try to be right.
- Be polite, and always tell him you had an excellent time. Be grateful. But don't follow up after the date by text or leave a long voicemail. Remember, that's a man's job; *and*
- Sit back and let him take the lead.

Don't Try to Convince a Man You're the One

A girl with no identity of her own may try to convince a man she is the right one for him. Not the girl who gets the guy, she is entirely comfortable in her skin. She'd rather dance on nails than mold herself into a woman she is not to keep a man by her side. She doesn't make modifications to her appearance, change her interests or opinions to appease anyone. She remains true to her authentic self even when a man is in her life.

If there are aspects of her life that don't mesh with who she is dating, she will not suppress her feelings or modify who she is. If her idea of *outdoorsy* is cocktails on the porch, you won't see her pitch a tent in the woods. If she doesn't drink, you won't catch her with a cold one in hand. If she prefers a five-star hotel, she won't agree to weekends tucked away in an RV.

Many women, sometimes unknowingly, begin to duplicate the exact behavior the man they are involved with is doing. If he's a lawyer, she becomes the perfect lawyer's wife. If he loves to fish, fishing becomes her great love. If he has a band, she follows him from dive to dive and becomes his manager.

In the romantic comedy *"Runaway Bride,"* Julia Roberts is cast as "Maggie," a woman who has run away from three weddings but is hoping not to do so on her fourth wedding attempt. Richard Gere is cast as "Ike," a New York City news reporter who sets out to write an article about Maggie, but in the process of doing so, falls in love with her.

During his research for the story, Ike realizes that Maggie alters her interests to mimic those of her fiancés to please them. This is signified most prominently by her choice of eggs, which changes with each husband-to-be.

So let me ask you, "How well do you know yourself?" "What do you love to do?" "What makes you happy?" "What do you do to relax?" "What is your decorating style?" "What are your interests?" "What are your passions?" "What does it take for you to be the best version of you, every single day?" In short, "How do you like your eggs?"

A self-assured woman carries with her a high level of peace and contentment that comes with having discovered herself. She's an expert in learning what pleases her, so she continues to live a happy life. She knows by making herself a priority; she will not become what someone else wants her to be, or worse, invisible.

The Way To A Man's Heart Is
Through His Stomach...

Please don't roll your eyes at this one. I'm very aware of what year it is. I know that since the 19th Century, strong, amazing women have broken barriers, so you and I have a right to vote, reproductive rights, and the right to work for equal pay. The results of their dedication, hard work, and determination have not only changed the lives and laws of women, but they have also paved the way for Ms. Suzie Homemaker to flourish into Ms. Independent. And Ms. Independent doesn't cook. But if the way to a man's heart happens to pass through the kitchen of an intelligent, witty, beautiful, no-nonsense modern-day, independent woman – All the better.

I'll make a confession... Had I never had children, I would have happily been the "order takeout" kind of girl for life. But age makes us all the wiser and now, speaking as a wife, a mother of two boys and a steppy to three more, I can attest to this: The Y-Chromosome loves food. Food makes men happy, happy, happy. When it comes to cooking, I finally decided since I couldn't beat them, I'd join them. It makes a complete difference as they're just happier with a full stomach.

You may have heard your mother or grandmother say, "If you want a man to love you, you should feed him good food." Julia Child once said, "I think careful cooking is love, don't you? The loveliest thing you can cook for someone who's close to you is about as nice a valentine as you can give." Regardless of whether you believe cooking for a man is an act of love, or you will never step foot in the kitchen, the fact is men love food.

The good news is if you can't cook, it's not a deal-breaker.

When a man loves a woman, he won't leave you high and dry because you can't boil water. However, men consider women who can cook, marriage material for one simple reason…It means one day when they are married and have children who are banging their forks and spoons on the table demanding something to eat; he'll know they're taken care of. Which is how men express and show their love…by providing and caring for their loved ones.

Nowadays, it's not even necessary to cook from scratch. After I married, I met a fantastic woman named Debbie, who owns a charming bistro, appropriately named "Debbie's Bistro." In the corner of the dining area, she placed two large commercial freezers stocked with 'ready to heat,' casseroles, dips, and vegetables. She makes delicious, southern homemade chicken spaghetti, lasagna, king ranch chicken, and anything else you can think of and places them in aluminum foil to-go containers. To prepare: Preheat oven to 350 degrees; Place casserole in the oven for one hour, serve with a salad or your favorite bread. She charges fifteen dollars for each, and frankly, I feel like she's short-changing herself. She can't prepare the dishes fast enough before 'time-deprived' women buy them up. I keep a shelf in my freezer stocked full of these clever casseroles for nights when I'm too busy to stop what I'm doing to take an hour or more to cook our meals. My husband and kids don't care where the food comes from; they're just happy when their bellies are full.

Another friend of mine takes her own casserole dish to her favorite Italian restaurant and asks them to prepare lasagna and passes it off as her own. The only thing she must do to cook dinner is to place the dish in the oven. She's been doing this for years, and to this day, her husband thinks she slaves away in the kitchen, making his favorite dish from scratch.

If you are challenged in the kitchen, become familiar with the grocery stores in your city and see what they have to offer. Most all sell prepared food you can arrange on your favorite dishes and serve on that special night. Don't forget to check out all of the tasty desserts.

WHEN TO DISH IT OUT

Before you break out the pots and pans and stock all his favorite foods in your pantry, *slow down*. Just as making him wait for sex is beneficial to you, in the beginning, making him wait for a home-cooked meal shows him you are not trying to win him over by showing off your domestic skills in the kitchen.

After the first month, invite him over for dinner and show off your cooking chops. If you can't cook, order take-out. Remove food from containers, arrange on your favorite serving dishes, and Taaadddaaa...Dinner is served! Just like your love, he will appreciate your efforts in the kitchen, so much more after he has earned it. From this point on, anything you bring to the table will be the best dinner he's ever had.

When you are too eager to do *wifely* duties such as clean his house, do his laundry, and cook dinner, he knows you're in it to win it. He believes you are using a perfectly grilled filet mignon as bait to lure him down the aisle. He'll take the bait and run -- *after he's had dessert*. In the interim stick to take-out and fine dining in restaurants. Don't forget a sweet kiss before you send him home hungry for more.

Chapter 8

Why He May Not Be Calling

"Being jealous of a beautiful woman is not going to make you more beautiful." –

Zsa Zsa Gabor

In its very healthiest form, insecurities force us to become our very best and keep us modest and humble. In its worst form, insecurities bring out fear, stress, anxiety, and the constant worry of the unknown. Fear makes the best women act irrational, insecure, and cynical. Women become messy when they act on emotions. When they become uncertain and full of doubt, their feelings take over and consume their minds.

Without a solid frame of reference, your imagination can take a life form on its own. When in doubt, insecurities take control of your mind and allow your thoughts to run wild because a man doesn't respond to a text quick enough for your liking. Reacting negatively too hastily makes you appear irrational and unattractive.

A Woman Who Is Without Jealousy Allows Her Inner Beauty and Confidence to Radiate

Jealousy is often a reflection of inadequacy and insecurity. A confident woman, comfortable in her skin, isn't jealous of other beautiful women, in fact, she compliments them and helps them whenever she can. If a strong woman sees another woman struggling, she offers her support and helps to lift her up. A secure woman knows insulting other women only makes her look petty, insecure, and small.

There will always be women who are more beautiful than you are. How you define your beauty is up to you. You can be a beautiful woman who has no class, no moral compass, possessive and controlling, and you will always pale in comparison to the mediocre woman who rocks it utterly comfortable in her skin. A woman who can only make conversation while making offhand comments about another woman's body shape, size, or choice of attire proves to a man she is superficial and classless.

Remember the old advice your mother or grandmother gave you? "If you don't have anything nice to say, don't say anything at all." Or, "If you can't be kind, be quiet." Are you a gossiper? Do your words tear people down? Are you critical or disrespectful? Consider how speaking poorly about anyone makes you appear. It makes the most beautiful women seem unattractive and small.

Don't Be a Negative Nellie

Some women look for things to go wrong. If her husband or boyfriend is thirty-minutes late coming home from work, she may jump right into interrogation mode. He'll immediately become defensive and think you've lost your mind. The same applies if you are overly attached. Men want to know you care; however, if your caring is expressed by wanting him to account for every waking minute of every waking day, it will be just like placing a large pillow over his head to suffocate the life out of him.

Keep in mind there is a difference between jealousy and suspicion. Often what breeds insecurity is a lack of clarity, doubt, and distrust. When a man doesn't give you the clarity you need to be content and happy, then it's high time to let him know the relationship is about to end, without hesitation.

Stop Obsessing About What He's Thinking, And Pay Attention to What He's Doing

When you must ask a man, "What are you thinking," or "What's on your mind?" And they continually dodge the question, take a step back and ask yourself what his behavior and actions are telling you. Does he say he misses you but never makes plans to see you? Unless he's enlisted in the military serving overseas, you can interpret that to mean he doesn't miss you *too* much. Because if he missed you, he would find a way to see you.

Does he initiate calls or texts? Does he tell you he loves you but never makes plans to see you? This means he doesn't value your relationship, nor does he make you a priority *because* he's not making an effort.

Is he no longer interested in sex? Is he under so much stress from work, school, building a house, saving orphaned children, or busy in another area of his life? If so, be supportive. If not, chances are there is another woman.

Does he say, "I love you," but your intuition is telling you this is not the way love is supposed to be? If so, don't waste your breath on an interrogation, instead, say, "This isn't working for me." Nicely, calmly and sweetly relay what changes need to be made to give you the clarity you need to make you happy. Give him time to fix the problem, and mentally prepare yourself to leave if the situation does not improve. There is no need to beat a dead horse, no further conversation is required.

Remember, ask once for what you want, you can even throw out a friendly reminder a second time, but under no circumstances should you have to ask for anything a *third* time. Repetitive questioning is what creates a nag. And if you are a constant nagger, he's probably learned to tune you out. When a man loves and cares for you, he takes the time *to* make time, to do whatever is needed to make you happy.

But He Said He Loved Me!

Sharon Stone once said, "Women might be able to fake orgasms, but men can fake whole relationships." Weeding out the horny toads from the men with good intentions can be problematic in that players can be very hard to identify. Players are *players*. Pretending you are the love of their life is no problem at all for the seasoned player. He might be making four other women feel the same way. He knows exactly what to say, and knows you are hanging on his every word.

The one thing the charming player lacks is patience. A player may try for a month or two, but anything longer is wasting his precious time, which could be best used on another *victim*. If you are taking things slow, he'll get the silent message you're not a woman who settles for basement bargains in the love department.

He Just Stopped Calling

Perhaps you committed the cardinal sin of *assuming*, which made your commitment-ready man run for the hills. A grave mistake many women make in the beginning stages of dating is assuming that you and Mr. Maybe are exclusive, thereby making him your boyfriend, right? Wrong. This assumption could be precisely why he is not texting, calling, or making dates as he used to. He was going with the flow, enjoying the good life from one day to the next, when all-of-a-sudden you changed the terms. You threw a monkey wrench into his system, and now he's all screwed up.

There are right ways and wrong ways to go from casual dating to having a dedicated man without him becoming icy and detached. Problems arise when you begin to treat him like he is your boyfriend, which he will always believe has happened all too quickly. Just because you have decided you want an exclusive, committed relationship doesn't mean he shares your same views.

A man wants and needs to feel as though he has won your heart through his pursuing, chasing, and wooing. If he feels forced into a relationship, he feels resentment, which will make him back away. If you do all the hard work for him, he won't feel like the man. Subconsciously, he feels he isn't in control. You presented no challenge, which gave him nothing to work for to win you over.

A man wants to put forth the effort to win your heart. Be a challenge. Don't be so obtainable and stand so still, a turtle could catch you. Give him the victory of winning you over.

Desperate for Love

Don't be so desperate you come off as pathetic. If you find yourself making declarations like, "I can't live without you," "You complete me," or "I don't know what I would do, if you ever left me," you've lost. *That's it, game over.* A man may not bolt out of the door at that moment, but you can bet he's planning an escape or waiting for something better to come along.

Happiness is a state of mind, not a person. When a man feels your happiness depends on whether he is in your life or not, the fear will make his hands tremble. It places too much pressure on him. Once you come to terms with the fact you and only you can push your happiness buttons, the planets will align, and all will fall perfectly into place.

Chapter 9

Why Financial Independence Wins His Heart

and Your Freedom

"People think at the end of the day that a man is the only answer [to fulfillment]. Actually, a job is better for me."

— Princess Diana

Ann Cotton hit the nail on the head when she so eloquently said, "Money is hardly neutral. Its connection to power makes it a highly charged social phenomenon and a mediator of relationships. Because men have historically controlled the money, it has given them a tool for controlling women." When I lived with my parents, they would say to me, "As long as you live in our house, under our roof, you have to abide by our rules." They had control over me and *rightfully* so. A man may never come right out and say it, but when your only source of unearned income is provided by him, he may handle you like a puppet. And what are you to do if he cuts the puppet strings? Having financial independence means no one ever has that kind of control and influence over you. Happiness, choices, power, security, control, independence, and freedom are just a few of the perks of having your own currency.

A self-made woman is a happy woman because relying on herself brings her joy. She is not content with asking for permission to buy something. She realizes her financial stability is not contingent upon whether a man is in her life or not. She is perfectly capable of budgeting for a household, buying a car, and takes good care of her credit. She is bright enough to make smart financial decisions, even on a shoestring budget. And this is the woman who has a man's respect from the get-go because he knows his money isn't keeping her by his side.

A Smart Woman Never Lets What a Man Brings to The Table the Only Thing She Has to Eat

David Back, the author of _Smart Women Finish Rich,_ wrote: "It's neither safe nor practical to assume that a man in your life can be counted on to take care of your finances." Regardless if you are happily married or still on the lookout for Mr. Right, you are ultimately responsible for knowing every aspect of your financial life. One smart rule to live by: always keep enough money stashed away to move out and establish a place of your own whether you need to or not. If you don't have a few bucks put away, start now. You should never have to stay where you don't want to be merely because you can't afford to move elsewhere.

Marilyn Monroe once commented, "If there is one thing in my life I am proud of, it's that I've never been a kept woman." How comfortable would you be handing financial control of your life over to one person? Would you decline a little single piece of paper that reads "Pay to the Order of," which gives you financial security, and independence, for love?

The self-made woman has traded the "Pretty Woman" fantasy of being rescued by a successful businessman in a white limousine with her dreams of owning a home, having a successful career, or running her own business. And men couldn't be happier. A man wants to know you want his love, not his money. If he sees you're not responsible with your own money, he won't trust you with his. He wants to know you're responsible.

A man finds the self-made woman who appreciates and values hard-earned money of her own, ever so appealing. One businessman I know ended his relationship with a high-maintenance trust fund baby. He said she threw tantrums when life didn't go her way, expected everyone to fix her problems, and drop whatever they were doing when she called in need of something. Months later, in walked a down-to-earth woman who continually tried to improve her life financially for the better. She paid her way and didn't wait for handouts. When a stressful situation arose, she proved she was a problem solver. He married her a year later.

A Real Man of Value Doesn't Want a Brainless Gold Digger Who Trades Sex for Money and The High-End LifeStyle

Gold diggers will always exist, and there will always be men who want a beautiful, living accessory on their arm. These couples are being replaced by the power couple, where both are intellectual equals, smart, savvy, and successful.

When Bernie Madoff's fifty-billion-dollar Ponzi scheme hit Actors Kevin Bacon and his wife, Kyra Sedgwick, the two didn't let the devastating financial loss destroy their marriage. Instead, they rolled their sleeves up and went to work. She later commented, "We ride the roller coasters together - the high highs and the low lows."

An Independent Woman Who Is Smart, Sexy and Sweet Is the Icing on The Cake

If you believe your independence and career-driven mind is the very thing men are turned off by, think again. Self-made women who have a strong-willed personality who project confidence enthrall a man's attention, and his heart. For decades women have classified themselves as being too unapproachable. When justifying why they are not married, a woman may say, "Men are intimidated by smart, financially successful women." They explain to themselves they are *too* intimidating for men to date because man after man, date after date, ultimately never pans out.

Women believe men feel weakened and put off by financially strong women who make their way for fear of losing significance as men. Some women think men are less attracted to a woman who can go neck to neck when it comes to the balance of the checkbook. But today, men have high regard for women who have financially thrived. They appreciate women who are accomplished, intelligent, and show strength when faced with adversity. One man said, "I highly respect my wife because she is capable in multiple roles -- a kickass Executive by day and a loving mother, wife, lover, and friend by night. All these qualities make her more appealing and sexier."

In an interview with ET, George Clooney told Nancy O'Dell, the reasons he fell in love with his wife, Amal. He said, "She's an amazing human being. She's caring. And she also happens to be one of the smartest people I've ever met." "I'm always very proud of her when I see her speaking at the International Court of Appeals in Strasbourg, you know, with her robe on. It's very impressive." There are several keywords in his interview, but the one that stands out: Proud. He could have spoken about her unquestionable beauty but instead focused on her intelligence.

What Stops a Man Dead in His Tracks?

Is when a woman brings her boss like brashness into the relationship. He doesn't want to feel as though he comes home to an unfriendly supervisor who monitors or micro-manages his every move. He wants a ladylike woman who lets him be king of his castle.

Do you remember the scene in *A Few Good Men* when Tom Cruise's character Daniel Kaffee and JoAnne Galloway, played by Demi Moore, were having dinner? Galloway reads off her successful resume to Kaffee and quickly follows up with... "I have two medals and two letters of commendation." Kaffee looks puzzled and responds, "Why are you always giving me your resume?"

Leading with a list of accolades may work in the workforce, but in the love department, you must understand you are not applying for a job. Remember, a successful career is something to be admired, but you can't share dinner with it. Leading with accomplishments and good deeds gives the impression you are trying to prove to a man you are smarter than he is and trying to *convince* him of why he should be dating you.

A Few Ways to Play Up Your Femininity

- Let him be a gentleman.
- Let him open doors.
- Let him spoil you.
- Let him take care of you.
- Let him fix something.
- Leave the corporate attire in the closet and dress up for him in feminine clothing.
- Let him plan the date and make reservations.
- Don't offer to pay for dinner. (Don't even reach for your purse when the waiter brings the check.)
- Don't always try to be right. Be a good sport, and humbly agree to disagree.
- Have good manners and always tell him you had a very good time. Be grateful.
- Let him take the lead; and
- Don't follow up after the date. Remember, that's his job.

As modern-day women, we have adapted to taking care of life on our own. Without realizing it, we forget to ask, much less expect someone to help us out. We handle everything perfectly fine, and sometimes we stay on automatic pilot. We forget men revel in helping, problem-solving, and doing things to help us out. It's in their DNA. When a man does something to help you out, it feeds his ego in a good way.

If you are too strong, proud, and independent and verbally voice the fact *you don't need a man, odds* are he will eventually find a woman who does. When women are competitive, argumentative, controlling, and always feel the need to be right, it turns a man off faster than you can flip a switch. A man wants to be in the company of a warm, caring, feminine woman. When you present yourself in a masculine way, it's unappealing to the male mind. I know… you can do anything a man can do – better, wearing stilettos. All you need is a high-heel and a butter knife. Right? The question you must ask yourself and answer honestly is: Are you too independent for your own good?

How to Make
A Man Feel as Handy as A Shirt Pocket

- On a cold night, ask him to build a blazing fire or light the gas fireplace.

- Have a pet? On cold or rainy mornings, ask him to take your four-legged pet out for a walk. If your pet brings you a present like dead rodents, ask him to carry off and dispose of the dearly departed.

- You know that hard to reach place in the middle of your back that is impossible to scratch? A problematic dress zipper when you are in a hurry? A necklace clasp? A man can solve all these problems with his steady hand.

- Need confirmation you look beautiful? All you need to do is ask how you look. A man is an instant confidence booster as he has no problem letting you know how stunning you look, every single time.

- Ask him to put together an at-home assembly project.

- Are you living by the light of your cell phone because it is too troublesome to change a lightbulb? Ask him to switch them out for you.

- Too tired to drive? A good man always takes the wheel. If you are among the directionally challenged women (myself included), the real alpha male will get you exactly where you need to be, fifteen minutes early. Not only are they good for driving and directions, but a good one will also take the liberty of filling your car with fuel. This comes in extremely handy during a rainstorm or when temperatures drop below forty-five degrees.

- Watching television is also better when you have a strong shoulder to rest your pretty head. A man turns into the voice of reason while watching sad movies like *"My Dog Skip."* While you are crying uncontrollably, he will quickly reassure you no dog was harmed while making the film.

- During the Christmas holidays, a man can prove himself to be invaluable. While you are lying on the sofa watching *Miracle on 34th Street,* ask him to retrieve the Christmas tree stored in the attic along with all the decorations stored in boxes.

- In the kitchen, you will find the aid a man can provide you second to none. He can reach those dishes stored in the top cabinets with ease. The jelly jar lid, which is so tight you just know it must have been secured with superglue, will open effortlessly with his aid. And let's not forget those pesky corks in wine bottles that will not budge. He'll be able to remove the cork with just a string and his bare hands.

And for enlisting his help to do any of the tasks mentioned above, what he wants in return is a sweet kiss and to hear the words, "Thank you, I appreciate you so much." Now, how hard is that?

Men Chasing Six String Dreams and
the Women Who Follow

There are desolate, well-off women who uphold family values to the highest, and for them, marriage is not only vital, it is also the only defining moment they will ever experience. Even today, there are still women who are desperate for love and marriage (not necessarily in that order). They believe by being married, they will be valued. This state of mind makes them live bait for the starving gigolo.

One story that stood out more so than others was that of a man I'll refer to as Mr. Freeloader, (because that's what I call men who let women pay their way) who met the epitome of what most consider the insecure woman. She created drama at every turn; she suffered from petty insecurities, behavioral disorders, childlike jealousies, anxiety, and an overall lack of confidence.

Despite her self-confessed inadequacies, she couldn't run off a man with green in his eyes, because what she did have in her favor was the financial generosity of her parents and a substantial child support check from a previous marriage. Mr. Freeloader, couldn't settle down with a woman who could easily support them both fast enough. Free money was hard to turn down, and he found a warm bed and a willing woman too cozy of a deal to pass up. He felt like he had finally reached the mountaintop, having landed a woman with a source of revenue and a house in move-in condition. He had no problem 'settling' for her because he was too comfortable sitting back in the La-Z-Boy while she, the financial gift from God, signed the checks and called the shots.

At first, she had no problem keeping a tight leash around his neck because he had no other options -- *at that time*. He wanted a piece of the good life and didn't mind taking money from babies to finance his six-string dreams. In her best effort to transform him from homeless to a Rhine-Stone Cowboy, she cleaned him up as best as she could with a full man makeover. She went over the top buying all the latest top-notch equipment to transform his garage band hobby into a country music band on the rise. In return, he stood by her side as she tried to recapture the fountain of youth. When her weight reached an all-time high, she scheduled weight-loss surgery to make her look as young as the man she married.

In the end, Mr. Freeloader could only remain on puppet strings for so long before frustration, unhappiness, and rebellion reared its hideous head. He left her high and dry, for a younger version, after all her hard work.

Had this woman worked just as hard following her dreams, pursuing her passions and achieving her goals when Mr. Freeloader left, she would have had something other than her parents to fall back on.

There will always be men who enter a relationship purely for their economic benefit. They leech off vulnerable women who are otherwise blindsided by love who are incapable of seeing they are being used for money until they are no longer needed. So, beware of leading with your pocketbook and falling for promises and potential before seeing if one can provide actual results.

Date a Man with a Plan

A smart woman knows a failure is not her equal, and she won't dumb herself down just for the sake of being in a relationship. Regardless if a man is established or not, she expects him to have a plan in place. Some may say it seems like this woman is all about money. *Nonsense.* She is all about stability and dependability, which are assets women and men alike find ever-so-attractive. Being a self-made man, or able to stay employed is a sign of reliability. It shows he is responsible and will one day be able to provide for a family on his own.

If you come across a man who does not have the financial means to date you, who is working toward his goals, it's crucial you let him be the man and compensate in other areas. Remember, dating is about learning who the man is, his goals, his ambitions, his dreams. If he is finding his way in the world, his actions must match his plans.

He may feel that because you hold the pen to the pocketbook, you have all the power. This can be emasculating to a man who has a Texas-size ego. It is imperative he pays for and plans the dates. If he asks what you would like for dinner, suggest something other than an expensive restaurant. You can also recommend dates that do not cost a cent.

If he doesn't blink an eye while planning dates and vacations on your pretty penny, you should consider this to be a big yellow warning flag waving for your attention to plan your exit, sweetly and swiftly.

A man worth a grain of salt will take the lead and not only be a man but a gentleman. When a man doesn't earn as much, he picks up in other areas. He makes important decisions, he opens doors, holds umbrellas, offers his coat when you are cold, and makes sure he takes care of you. He may not be able to provide you financial security, but he should make up for it in other areas. Women have more than just financial needs, so make sure he is pulling his weight in different ways.

Why Smart, Pretty Women Get Discarded

Smart, successful women become baffled when a man ends a relationship with her for another woman who is not as successful or as pretty. The first question she will ask is, "Why is he with that bitch and not me? I'm prettier, smarter, and more successful." Men will quickly tell you it has nothing to do with her beauty or accomplishments, but more with her personality, her sense of humor, and her laid-back spirit. It comes down to how a woman makes a man feel. And a man wants a woman that makes him feel damn good.

Accomplishments women achieve are considered bonuses, not guarantees of 'happily ever after.' At the end of the day, a man must feel admired, needed, and appreciated, *along* with emotional attraction. As we have lists of the quality's men must have, men may not write it down on paper, but they have a mental list of requirements and negotiables as well. They have a strong desire to find a woman who possesses a strong work ethic, morals, and one who has a vision for her future.

Certain qualities matter to men because he feels a connection to women who are well rounded, intelligent, and have independent goals of her own. He may not care precisely what your goals are, but he wants to know they exist. Even if her sole objective is to raise a family, he will appreciate her love of family if he too, is family-minded. It takes a lot to be an 'Executive of Household Affairs.' At the end of the day, he wants to be assured you will be content even when he's not by your side.

If you meet his list of requirements and negotiables, the rest comes down to chemistry and attraction. He won't stay with you just because you're successful. Take Gwen Stefani's ex-husband, who had an affair with their nanny. Who, *by the way*, was no Gwen Stefani. If a man isn't attracted to you, the fact you have a Ph.D., or a Star on the Hollywood Walk of Fame is of no significance. Just as beauty won't keep a man by your side. There must be a physical attraction present. Your success, career, and dreams will enhance your appeal, but they won't seal the deal.

You must understand men have a degree of insecurity on a level we cannot begin to comprehend. It comes down to how men feel when they are with a woman, not how much she brings to the table. Men want to feel like men. They want to feel needed and, more importantly, wanted, and appreciated. The day you wound his fragile ego, is the day you should throw in the white towel and surrender.

In the relationship arena, men want balanced input proving their opinions are just as important, especially when it comes to making big decisions. If you bypass this, you take his alpha male card. At their core, men are providers, hunters, and gatherers. A woman's happiness motivates a man to better himself. If you don't put your pride to the side and find a way for him to be the man, feel like a man, and act like a man, he'll eventually find someone else who can.

Chapter 10

Learn to Say 'No' Without Explanation

"The art of leadership is saying no, not saying yes. It is very easy to say yes."

— Tony Blair

Vanessa Bohns explained, "People think that they'll be OK saying no, but in the moment, when you're actually face-to-face with someone, and you're in this awkward, embarrassing, sort of guilt-ridden experience, you don't realize that it's overpowering, and you're more likely to give in and say yes." As women, we continually over-commit ourselves regardless of the havoc it wreaks on our lives. The standards we hold ourselves to are really ridiculous at times. No man would fill their plate with what we do in a day, week, or month. We must liberate ourselves from saying *yes* to each and every request made of us.

Women have been programmed to be as sweet as a glass of southern iced tea since birth. We have been raised to please and nurture. If we say no, we feel as though we are slapping someone across the face. When it comes to relationships, some women are just so happy to be in one, they don't want to stir the pot by saying no for fear of letting someone down or being rude.

You must acquire the ability to give yourself permission to use the two-syllable word "no," guilt free. Teaching yourself to say no in a non-bitchy, non-threatening way is indeed the best gift you can ever give yourself. Learning to say no the right way will set you free from regret, worry, anxiety, and a host of other emotions.

A confident woman has not only learned to say no, but she has also mastered it. So many women, myself included, feel as though we are obligated to say yes to everyone and every request made of us even though saying yes often makes us feel overwhelmed or resentful. We fear that telling someone no will come off as cold-hearted, ill-mannered, or will ultimately hurt their feelings. We are so scared if we say no to a man, it will ruin our chances of a future with him.

There are plenty of *yes* girls in the world. If you want to set yourself apart from the herd and earn a little admiration in the process, let the word no roll off your tongue until it becomes as natural as saying other words, such as "please" and "thank you." If you are too nice and accommodating, you'll be considered a doormat, a woman without a spine. If you are too harsh, you're considered a bitch, but when you can learn to say *no* without being rude, brash, short, or cold, …that's when you have found the sweet spot. "Yes girls" make a man happy for a little while, but the woman who can say no without flinching, she's the one who wins his respect.

When the word no comes from the lips of a woman in a way

that is just as smooth and sweet as apple pie moonshine, it tells a man she is the one who holds the reigns. It proves you won't be a pushover. Being comfortable using the word no tells a man you have limits, which confirms you are a woman who isn't afraid to set boundaries.

Start now and mentally prepare yourself for the next time you are face to face in a situation where you will be required to say no. Before mother-nature automatically speaks on your behalf and agrees by saying yes, stop and reflect on how you feel about deciding to do what you are being asked to do?

Does it make you feel helpful, pleased, and excited? Or, does it make you feel inconvenienced and overwhelmed? Does it take away time you would rather spend with your family, friends, or even yourself? By saying yes, does it overextend you? If any of the latter is true, then it is time to learn two letters. *The N and the O.* When saying no, hopefully, the result you would like to have, is the person who is receiving the no, to feel appreciated, and respected. When delivered correctly, saying no is far from callous. *How* you say, no is more significant than the no itself. Make sure when you say no, it's stated with sincerity, not bitchiness. Unless of course, bitchiness is warranted.

May I Use You for The Night?

My favorite is the man who calls or sends a text message on a Friday night, wanting a date in just a few hours. Just as smooth as silk, change the terms of his request. "Tonight, is not good for me, Wednesday after work is much better." And then go silent and wait for his response. If he doesn't respond to your message, there is no need to send a follow-up. He got your message. He's provided you with all the information you need to know.

By changing his request pleasantly, you did not turn him down; you only made it more convenient for yourself. In a non-nagging, non-bitchy way, you sent two messages loud and clear. The first message being he should make plans sooner. The second message is you are not the last-minute midnight call girl. Some men are slower than others to catch on, and it could take several times of you changing the terms. Hang in there; he will eventually get it. The next time he calls for a date, he will do so well in advance.

A Little Tweak Here And There

In some situations, we bite off more than we can chew and agree to requests, which are far too much for us to handle. They're just too large for us to add to our ever-full plate. Sometimes a request is just too inconvenient and is sought at an inopportune time. In this situation, again, you adjust the request to fit your needs.

Let's say at the last minute, he suggests you cook dinner after work instead of going out to a restaurant. Doing so means you would have to fight your way through rush hour traffic, go to the grocery store to buy everything you need to make dinner. Once you get home, it could take another hour to prepare. Once you finally sit-down, chances are you may be too tired to enjoy it. Add another thirty to forty-five minutes cleaning the kitchen. Once that chore is done, you take a bath and fall face-first into bed.

Learn how to say no by adjusting the request made of you by making it more convenient for you to do. Instead of agreeing to make a four-course meal from scratch, order take-out instead. *(Note: Take out of to-go containers and place on your best dishes.)* Mission accomplished!

Saying *No*, Does Not Mean *No* Forever, Just *No* Right Now

Another way women bend over backward to accommodate men is by agreeing to last-minute plans. My friend Samantha explained she was running errands after her morning workout when her boyfriend called her cell phone. He asked if she could swing by a local restaurant to meet him and his mother, who was in town for lunch.

Samantha dropped what she was doing, rushed home to shower and dress, and then hurried to the restaurant only to discover they had not only started lunch but had also finished without her.

Would anyone have died if she would have said, "I can't make it right now, how about dinner tonight?" No, there would have been no casualties. Boyfriend and his mother would have had an excellent lunch, Samantha would have finished her errands and would not have been rushed to get dressed and to the restaurant. Saying no does not mean no forever, just no right now.

Hell No

On the other hand, it is entirely acceptable just to say no. I don't know who said it first, but my favorite go-to line is, "Never complain, never explain." You don't owe anyone an excuse or explanation. No means no.

If you've been a casualty of poor treatment, disrespect, and bad behavior, consider yourself on the road to recovery by learning to say no. Over time you'll become more and more comfortable with the word. Step by little step, you will notice you are no longer being taken for granted, and your self-esteem will soar. One little word protects you while teaching the man in your life a valuable lesson about respect and courtesy.

There are many times in your life when it is necessary to protect yourself from being hurt and used, just by saying, "No."

Need help practicing? Let me help you. Repeat the following out loud.

- "No, tonight isn't good for me."
- "No, this is not okay with me."
- "No, this is not something I can overlook."
- "No, this doesn't work for me."
- "No, this is not acceptable."
- "No, that would be an inconvenience for me."
- "No, I can't do that, but what about this…"
- "No, thank-you."
- "No;" and
- "Hell No." (My favorite)

If you need help, practice in front of a mirror. You'll be able to see yourself in real time, gauge your effectiveness, and make instant alterations. *Don't forget to smile.*

Confident and Carefree

One characteristic that is just as important as *confidence* is your capability to go with the flow, be easygoing and laidback. If you were to ask your ex-boyfriends or closest girlfriends to rate you as 'demanding' or 'amiable,' which one would they choose?

I just told you I want you to have a backbone and stand up for yourself and say no when you are asked to do something you are uncomfortable with doing. I haven't changed my mind; I still want you to learn to say no. At the same time, if you say no to each request or suggestion that is made or given, a man will place you in the demanding and challenging category. If you're the type who must have your way all the time, or you can't deviate from plans now and then, he'll think you're just too much damn work.

I consider myself a yes person with limits. I have to make decisions each and every day that impact people. I want to be easygoing and accommodating when I can. On the other hand, when I say "no," I want them to hear me and understand, I am saying no for a reason, not just to be difficult. Being easygoing doesn't cost a cent and requires nothing more than a wish to have fun and eradicate unnecessary conflict and drama in your life and relationships. If you insist *everyone* do *everything* your way, all the time, you'll be labeled as *unreasonable*.

If you have so many self-imposed rules, you find yourself saying no all the time, a man will never know when to perk up and pay attention when something is *truly* important to you.

A man determines whether you're easygoing based on how you handle the small stuff. On the other hand, if you demand he conforms to all your likes, your suggestions, and your plans each time he will quickly, mentally file you under problematic, and sprint down the street.

Saying no all of the time will get you nowhere. A man wants to be himself around you, but if he feels every suggestion and idea is shot down because it's your way or the highway, eventually he'll choose the road which leads to an easygoing woman. Because 'difficult' makes him feel *inadequate* and *suffocated*. He may want to be with you, but he also wants to be himself. His whole world can't revolve around following your rules, any more than your world can or should revolve around his.

If relationships are about anything, they are about compromise. Not just getting your way. So, if you believe being right is more important than being happy, perhaps relationships aren't for you. But, you have the power of choice, and I hope you choose "easy going" for the simple reason I'm about to tell you... *Easy going women almost always get what they want because when something is important to them, a man in love will move mountains to give it to her.*

Chapter 11

What to Do When He's Slipping Away

"I'm one of those guys who believes that you need a strong woman in your life."

-- *Pierce Brosnan*

You once thought he worshiped the ground you walked on. Now you spend most of the day racking your brain trying to justify his standoffish behavior. You're confused. You thought all was going well. You thought he was as crazy about *you* as you were him. Right? You both were spending lots of time together. He was making future dates, calling, and texting every day and night. He showed you what it was like to be wined and dined, loved, and cared for.

Suddenly, as quick as a wink, things shifted, and he began to withdraw, or the worse, he vanished like Houdini. He left you wondering, "What in the hell just happened?"

There is good news and bad news, and I'll start with good news because I love to spread relationship cheer. The good news is, at times, men pull away just as a relationship begins to evolve.

A man views *commitment* as a considerable obligation. An obligation a real man does not take lightly. After all, the alpha male must have a plan in place to provide for and protect his woman. Perhaps he needs some time alone with his thoughts to develop a plan. This is excellent news for you. This means he loves you... He's caught feelings.

On the other hand, the fact he ceased calling, texting, and making plans with you can also mean he is moving in a different direction. When a man stops contacting you, you have several options. Before I list them, I can't emphasize the following enough... *Now is not the time to reveal your 'crazy' side.*

OPTIONS

Option 1: Do absolutely nothing. Become hard to reach. Cut off all forms of contact. A man expects you to call or text thirty times a day, asking, "Where the hell are you," and, "Why haven't you called?" Because he knows he is supposed to call, and he knows you're expecting him to call. When you don't, loud alarm bells start ringing, alerting his fragile ego. Chances are this should get his attention -- *if he cares for you.*

Option 2: Confront him. Ask him, "Is there anywhere else you'd like to be?" This makes it known you are very aware of the crap he's pulling, and you won't stand for it. This method, if done correctly: calm, cool, and collected, will earn his admiration and show him your backbone at the same time. Done incorrectly: emotionally, angry, spiteful, and clingy-- he'll classify you as crazy.

Option 3: Don't change a thing. Keep putting up with his shit. Be the woman he leaves in relationship limbo. Continue to be the doormat he walks all over. Stay in his rotation.

Imagine the kind of woman the man you are dating would consider being marriage material. In the description listed, I bet there will be one essential element: *Self Control*. Before you make the same mistake thousands and I do mean thousands, of women, have made by calling, texting, and sending up smoke signals desperately seeking closure. Know sometimes there is no closure. And efforts made trying to obtain closure come off as pathetic and desperate. Pathetic and desperate will keep you single and alone.

Visualize your next move carefully. Consider whether the thirty-seventh text message or voice mail will make more of an impression than the first one did. Sad and pitiful are not pretty colors to wear. The best reaction is no reaction at all. What men do hear is silence, and its louder than any words you can verbally voice.

Just Don't

➤ Call, text, or private message him. When men actively pursue women by calling, texting, and making plans, it is flattering and considered romantic. When women do it, it's *seen as an* act of desperation.

➤ Chase him down by visiting places he frequents or worse, stopping by his place of work. Doing so makes you appear to be psycho, pitiful, and a hot mess. And maybe you are, but he doesn't need to know this.

> ➢ Call and tell him you are never speaking to him again. He will realize this when you disappear and go silent like a submerged submarine.

> ➢ Stay in contact with his friends and family to keep tabs on his life. His life is not your life, and the less you know, the better off you'll be during the long hard road to recovery.

> ➢ No Ex-Sex. If your vagina couldn't keep Mr. Ex by your side, in the beginning, odds are one more orgasm won't change his mind. But he will take one last 'O' after midnight when he has nothing better to do.

Ultimately making desperate attempts alarms the hell out of well-rounded men. So, when he starts to withdraw, although you may be inclined to show him how much you care, what you should give him is the gift of time. Yes, that's right, do nothing and say nothing. Dialing his number will not help, sending nothing text messages, won't do the trick. When you must ask a man if he's still interested in you, chances are he is not. Regardless of how painful it is, consider it a favor you are doing him by allowing him space to sort out his feelings. Consider it a courtesy you are doing for yourself because there are two things you should be called while exiting a relationship, 'classy' and 'dignified.'

For a man to miss you, you must breathe, eat, and sleep the *No Contact Rule*. Let silence speak on your behalf. A man will never miss you if you are like a piece of toast in a toaster that pops up every three minutes. Throw yourself into work and hobbies. If you don't have a hobby – find one. Don't walk around with your phone in hand, praying to the phone gods to just make it ring. If you show him what a mess you can be when he needs space, you will only drive him further away.

A man will only miss you when he is under the impression you are gone for good. If he always knows you will be there waiting for him, like a loyal Golden retriever waiting at the door, regardless of how badly he messes up, or how far he strays, he will never feel the need to make an effort to be nearby. Just as in the game of poker, to win, you must establish early on, you're not afraid to lose.

At the end of the day, wouldn't it be better knowing he made the decision to pick up the phone to check on you? That he made an attempt to make plans to see you? That he has come to a conclusion on his own, his life is better with you in it? If out of desperation, you initiate the first move, you'll never know if he loved you enough to make an effort on his own. And you are worth every bit of effort.

Stop Begging. Stop Pleading. Stop Convincing.

Apologizing when a man has messed up is simply the biggest gaffe a woman can make. Stop apologizing when a man has made a mistake. When a man leaves you wondering, "What you did wrong?" Many women resort to crying and pleas for forgiveness for "whatever she did wrong." Through sobs, she may profess, "I can't imagine life without you," or, "What can I do to make you change your mind?" and "I'm sorry for whatever I did." At this point, he knows he could get by with murder. If you have to humiliate and demean yourself by begging for his love, know you are on the road to another doomed relationship. If he does *forgive* you and takes you back, you've given him the power and permission to continue to hurt you.

You may believe to change his mind, you only need to appeal to his sense of reason, and then everything will be okay. You want to offer an apology, even though you don't know why you are apologizing. You want to vow to do whatever it takes to improve the relationship you were not responsible for breaking. But, by offering change, an apology and promises to do better, when you did nothing wrong, you diminish your worth and lose your dignity in the process. The only thing you have accomplished is convincing him his decision to cut ties with you was hands down, the best choice he has ever made in his life.

If a man is *not* interested in you, nothing you do or say can get him to stay with you. You may believe once he sees the tears streaming down your beautiful face, he will change his mind, and you will receive a sympathetic change of heart. *Think again.* He will assume you have lost yourself in the relationship and are now co-dependent on him, which is equivalent to a needy fish. If you believe the only impression you make is the first impression, think of the lasting impression you are leaving while going a little insane because one man does not mutually share the same feelings. It's best to cry yourself a river and get on with it privately.

Men only try to contact you when they realize they have made a mistake by letting a secure, intelligent, confident woman slip through their grasp. When faced with a man making his exit, step aside to let him pass. Let him know he's not handcuffed to your wrist.

Chapter 12

How to Handle Relationship Limbo

"What a lovely surprise to finally discover how unlonely being alone can be."

- Ellen Burstyn

Relationship Limbo makes women insecure, needy, and a little crazy because, as women, we don't like the unknown. It makes one experience tremendous highs and unfathomable lows. We're creatures of habit who thrive on stability. We don't do well with indecision and uncertainty.

A fact is a man who adores you will never make you feel insecure. Instead, he will make you feel most at ease. You won't question his intentions because he always has your best interest at heart. He won't make you feel as though you're walking on eggshells, he won't make you feel anxious, and he won't make you question his love for you. You'll know when a man loves you because he never places a single doubt in your mind.

In Greg Behrendt's New York Times bestseller *He's Just Not*

That Into You, he handsomely explained the things you will never do when involved with a man who cares about you. He wrote, "You'll never see you staring maniacally at your phone, willing it to ring. You'll never see you ruining an evening with friends because you're calling for your messages every fifteen seconds. You'll never see you hating yourself for calling him when you know you shouldn't have. What you will see is you being treated so well that no phone antics will be necessary. You'll be too busy being adored."

SIGNS YOU ARE STUCK IN RELATIONSHIP LIMBO

- ✓ He does a disappearing act where he appears and disappears.

- ✓ He implies he cares for you, but his actions don't reflect it.

- ✓ He's not interested in what is going on in your life.

- ✓ He leaves you wondering what he's doing for days and weeks at a time.

- ✓ He sporadically calls or texts.

- ✓ He only makes you feel appreciated when he wants something from you…like sex.

- ✓ He speaks about the future, and you're not included.

- ✓ He doesn't make plans to see you in advance.

The most significant sign which conveys you are stuck in relationship limbo is what so many people call a woman's best friend. *Her intuition.* Some people, like me, refer to it as a whisper from God. Even if women are clueless, even if women have no common sense or street smarts, God has blessed them with intuition. When you are feeling apprehensive, scared, and don't know how to handle a problem you are facing in life or a relationship, find a place where you can be alone. Close your eyes and listen to what your intuitive sense is telling you to do.

Confident women have learned to trust their intuition and rely on all it is telling them. If you believe it and follow its wisdom, you won't go wrong. Where you go wrong is when you pay no attention to that little inner voice, that little feeling inside of you that makes your heart feel a little bit heavier. That small inner voice whispering, "Something's not right here."

Don't take living in relationship hell. It's really that simple. If you want clarity and are unable to get it, have the strength to walk away and provide your own sense of clarity. What other choice do you have? You can't make someone do something they're unwilling to do. You can't force someone to love you when they do not. And why would you try? Why would you want someone to be where they don't want to be? Pick up your purse and exit the premises at once. If he really loves you, there's no need to worry; he won't stay away for long. He'll eventually seek you out. All you can do is let him know you are unhappy with this arrangement, and you are not afraid to change it. Unless and until you are receiving what you want and deserve, you're going to be happy single. And maybe you'll be sad for a while, but I promise you will eventually be happy again. And being happy single is much better than being insecure, overwhelmed with uncertainty, and unhappy stuck in relationship hell.

A Vacation from The Dating Game

Audrey Hepburn once said, "I have to be alone very often. I'd be quite happy if I spent from Saturday night until Monday morning alone in my apartment. That's how I refuel." Marilyn Monroe whispered, "I restore myself when I'm alone." And Anne Frank, so eloquently wrote, "The best remedy for those who are afraid, lonely or unhappy is to go outside, somewhere where they can be quiet, alone with the heavens, nature, and God. Because only then does one feel that all is as it should be." For many women, being alone makes them feel lonely, unwanted, and unloved. But in truth, being alone for a while can be righteous for the soul.

If you've decided to make your exit after being stuck in relationship limbo, good for you! Now that you've removed the anxiety, confusion, and uncertainty a man may have caused you, due to a lack of commitment on his part, you will have one less problem in your life. This frees your mind from worries, stress, anxiety, and feeling like the weight of the world is on your shoulders. Unhealthy relationships can be mentally exhausting and will eventually drain you of your get-up-and-go. So, while having a boyfriend, husband, or lover may have its advantages, so does being a single lady.

Taking a dating sabbatical may be just what you need to recharge your mind and spirit. Embrace time spent alone. Learn to enjoy your company. When you rid your mind of worry, which consumes every minute of your day when you are in a dead-end relationship, great things in life begin to unfold.

For starters, your priority is no longer focused on keeping someone else happy. You are now dedicated to rediscovering what brings you joy. Gradually, you will feel your life sliding back on track once you begin to take time for self-reflection. When you are only processing your feelings and your thoughts, not those of others, the process of healing your heart and finding true happiness begins.

When you are involved in a relationship where you are always meeting the needs of another, we tend to forget about ourselves. We have no time to think about our needs. We spend so much of our lives catering to the needs of boyfriends, husbands, children, co-workers, and bosses that we forget to make our needs a priority. We forget that we have also been afforded the right to the pursuit of happiness. *Our happiness.*

If you are having trouble discovering who it is you are, weekends spent without following someone else's itinerary will give you time to devote to what you enjoy. You don't have to do or plan anything if that is what makes you happy. Think of a relaxing weekend where you don't apply makeup or wear a bra! *A win, win!* Catch up on the latest movies that have just been released. Take the first weekend to *rest, recharge,* and *revitalize* your mind.

The second weekend plan something *you* would like to do. Apply make-up, look your casual best, and try a new restaurant that sounds good. You don't have to settle for Mexican when you want Sushi because the decision is all up to you. Take a book or your Kindle and have a long lunch by yourself. Don't forget dessert.

Have you forgotten what your interests and hobbies are? There is no better time than now to modify your life to your needs. I know, it may almost sound like a foreign concept.

However, since you no longer have to compromise on what two people want, you have the sweet freedom of choice. Imagine for one minute how liberating it is to have no plans at all. If you're going to stay home and do nothing, no problem. Do you want to meet your girlfriends for a girl's night out? Done! Or spend the afternoon shopping? You're ready! You are now officially back in charge of your life.

When you embrace being alone and detach yourself from people who are bringing you down, you can begin to explore what you enjoy again. What is it you are doing when you find yourself most content? If you can identify what your strengths are and build on them, you can and will lead a happier existence. When you spend time alone, you can reflect on your past. What did you love to do before anyone told you what you should be doing? What is your definition of a great woman? Design a plan for your definition of, and destination to greatness.

Perhaps being in a relationship consumed your time, and you let yourself go. Maybe you let your house get out of order. Since your home is your haven, start there. Organize your home. Redecorate if sprucing things up will make you happy. The stack of bills you have been looking at for over a month, tackle them. Get them out of the way. When you can spend time alone, you can be more productive than ever. With your house in order and more time to focus on your life, relationships with friends and family will be ones you develop a greater appreciation for.

Alone time also makes you more self-reliant, confident, and independent. There is no second-guessing yourself, walking on eggshells, or apologizing for something you have just done. Once you're alone, the only person's happiness you will be concerned with is your own. Keeping others happy is no longer on your to-do list. Validation from others is no longer sought or necessary. Obtaining approval from friends, family, or a man before taking action is no longer warranted. Slowly you will begin to trust your instincts again, and your confidence will have no limits.

A woman who is just as happy, comfortable, and carefree on her own as she is with others is as appealing to a man as they come. She has discovered her authentic self and knows she is capable of being fully satisfied with or without a man by her side. It's not she doesn't want one. However, she wants someone who can bring a new level of happiness to her life. She wants a man to compliment her life, not complete it. Her emotional sanity and happiness are not contingent upon another person. And this is when and how the girl gets the guy.

Clingy vs. Confident

➤ The *Clingy* woman attempts to convince a man she's worthy. A *Confident* woman does nothing and expects a man to prove his worth to her.

➤ The *Clingy* woman tries to change a man. A *Confident* woman dates a man *as is*.

➤ The *Clingy* woman revolves her life around a man. A *Confident* woman has a life of her own.

➤ The *Clingy* woman chases a man. A *Confident* woman lets a man pursue her.

➤ The *Clingy* woman tolerates being treated like a doormat. A *Confident* Woman gets off the floor.

➤ The *Clingy* woman will live in relationship limbo. A *Confident* woman picks up her purse and leaves.

➤ The *Clingy* woman asks for everything. A *Confident* woman asks for *nothing* and receives everything.

➤ The *Clingy* woman must have a relationship to feel valued. A *Confident* woman knows her value and is just as happy by herself.

➤ The *Clingy* woman ignores warning signs. A *Confident* woman trusts her instincts and intuition.

➤ The *Clingy* woman is afraid to rock the boat for fear of conflict. A *Confident* woman will stand up for herself and voice her concern.

➤ The *Clingy* woman bends over backwards to keep a

man interested. A *Confident* woman sits back and lets a man persuade her.

➢ The *Clingy* woman believes she has to be sexy to keep a man. A *Confident* woman knows she has more to offer.

➢ The *Clingy* woman focuses on what a man says. A *Confident* woman focuses on his actions.

➢ The *Clingy* woman uses her body to get what she wants. A *Confident* woman uses her mind.

➢ The *Clingy* woman plays hard to get. The *Confident* woman *is* hard to get.

The Best Definition of Love...

I included this scripture at the end of my first book, Ignore the Guy, Get the Guy. I include it again, for no other reason than I believe it to be the most accurate, beautifully described definition of what any one person or dictionary could ever describe whether you are a believer or non-believer.

> *Love is patient and kind. Love is not jealous, boastful, proud, or rude. It does not demand its own way. It is not irritable, and it keeps no record of being wronged. It does not rejoice about injustice but rejoices whenever the truth wins out. Love never gives up, never loses faith, is always hopeful, and endures through every circumstance.*

> 1 Corinthians 13

Also by Leslie Braswell

Ignore the Guy, Get the Guy:

The Art of No Contact: A Woman's Survival Guide to Mastering a Breakup and Taking Back her Power

Bitch Up!

Expect More, Get More

A Woman's Guide to Maintaining Her Power and Sanity After a Breakup

About the Author

Leslie Braswell is a best-selling author who loves to empower women with knowledge when it comes to matters of the heart. She does so through favorite books like *Ignore the Guy, Get the Guy: The Art of No Contact: A Woman's Survival Guide to Mastering a Break-Up and Taking Back Her Power, How to Be the Girl Who Gets the Guy* and Bitch Up! Expect More, Get More. She loves to help women raise their confidence to be the best they can be in relationships and in life.

Made in the USA
Columbia, SC
23 October 2023

24839142R00070